"A short read for a long-term investment into the health and care of the most valuable, immortal parts of who we are. This is a life-changing truth and a must-read."

Tommy Barnett, global pastor, Dream City Church, Phoenix

"Historically, the church has devoted plenty of attention to spiritual things, but very little attention to emotional things. By delving deep into Gregory Dickow's new book, *Soul Cure*, you will begin to understand your true worth, unlock the secrets to soul health and unleash God's unfathomable grace in your life. You will learn to properly deal with emotional pain so you can be healed and free in your soul. This book can cure everything that ails you spiritually!"

Creflo Dollar, founder and senior pastor,
World Changers Church International

"This is a book of hope and laughter and life! Anyone who has faced loss, pain or hardship will find comfort and encouragement on every page."

Margaret Feinberg, author, *More Power to You: Declarations to Break Free from Fear and Take Back Your Life*

"Gregory Dickow offers readers a master class on restoring your soul, healing the storm from within and leading you to a breakthrough transformation. I believe that every bit of healing you need for your heart, your soul, your mind and your emotions—and every bit of healing needed in the world—starts in the pages of this book."

Ron Luce, cofounder, Generation Next

"There's healing for your mind, will and emotions—and it is found in Gregory Dickow's new book, *Soul Cure*. You will discover a shift in your focus from the negative to what is beautiful and how you can win the battle over loneliness, depression, anger, guilt and shame. When you read this book, you will realize once and for all that God will finish what He started in you—just like He promised. That your story is not over, it's still being written. What an incredible healing journey awaits you within these pages."

John Mason, author, *An Enemy Called Average* and numerous other bestselling books

"*Soul Cure* will revolutionize your mentality into a new dimension of understanding health and prosperity. Greg Dickow's gift in wisdom has revealed life-changing cure."

Dr. Stephan K. Munsey, co-pastor, Family Christian Center, Munster, Indiana; author, *Unleashing Your God-Given Dreams*

"*Soul Cure* is a necessary weapon in our arsenal against the enemy. Gregory Dickow takes readers through the journey of understanding the root causes of the spiritual forces behind human pain and suffering. Instead of simply offering advice to medicate the symptoms that cause spiritual attacks, he gives powerful navigational tools to dismantle the enemy's plot so that every believer can live in true freedom and victory."

John Ramirez, evangelist; author, *Conquer Your Deliverance: How to Live a Life of Total Freedom*

"Pastor Dickow defines the soul as 'your mind to think, your heart to feel and your will to decide.' Our souls are truly running the show, and for many of us the show has been something of a nightmare. This book is dedicated to helping us focus on what is beautiful. It's a wonderful book. Powerful and at times hilarious. Dickow is wise, loving, smart, funny and real. This is one to read and read again."

Susan Scott, author, *Fierce Love: Creating a Love That Lasts— One Conversation at a Time* and *Fierce Conversations: Achieving Success at Work and in Life, One Conversation at a Time*

SOUL
CURE

SOUL CURE

HOW TO HEAL YOUR PAIN
AND DISCOVER YOUR PURPOSE

GREGORY DICKOW

Chosen
a division of Baker Publishing Group
Minneapolis, Minnesota

© 2022 by Gregory Dickow Ministries

Published by Chosen Books
11400 Hampshire Avenue South
Minneapolis, Minnesota 55438
www.chosenbooks.com

Chosen Books is a division of
Baker Publishing Group, Grand Rapids, Michigan

Printed in the United States of America

Library of Congress Cataloging-in-Publication Data
Names: Dickow, Gregory, author.
Title: Soul cure : how to heal your pain and discover your purpose / Gregory Dickow.
Description: Minneapolis, Minnesota : Chosen Books, a division of Baker Publishing Group, [2022]
Identifiers: LCCN 2021051687 | ISBN 9780800762452 (cloth) | ISBN 9781493437184 (ebook)
Subjects: LCSH: Mental health—Religious aspects—Christianity. | Emotions—Religious aspects—Christianity. | Suffering—Religious aspects—Christianity. | Pain—Religious aspects—Christianity. | Vocation—Christianity.
Classification: LCC BT732.4 .D49 2022 | DDC 261.8/322—dc23/eng/20211118
LC record available at https://lccn.loc.gov/2021051687

This publication is intended to provide helpful and informative material on the subjects addressed. Readers should consult their personal health professionals before adopting any of the suggestions in this book or drawing inferences from it. The author and publisher expressly disclaim responsibility for any adverse effects arising from the use or application of the information contained in this book.

Copyright information continued on page 262.

22   23   24   25   26   27   28   7   6   5   4   3   2   1

Contents

Author's Note

As I sit here in the fall of 2021, the world is struggling mightily with an unprecedented pandemic that has ravaged millions; violence and terrorism around the world; weather disasters that have decimated cities and families—you name it.

So many of us are in pain. We are anxious and worried, perhaps not for ourselves as much as for our families and children. We feel insecure. Some even question their faith.

But as I ponder all this, I am reminded that there are two incredible gifts that should never be taken for granted: One is health—a precious yet fragile gift, which is a lesson we have all learned during the pandemic. The second gift may surprise you. In a simple word—adversity—conditions that continually challenge us and make us stronger and more resilient. In this way, life is a journey of discovery, an unfolding story playing out in real time, requiring us to bob and weave with destiny.

In my nearly thirty-year experience as pastor of Life Changers International Church, I have ministered to thousands of people and witnessed countless stories of trouble and pain. I have found that each of us is healing from something as we pursue wholeness—spirit, soul and body. Each of us is discovering something—the gifts, talents, desires and dreams we carry within us, just as a woman might carry a new life growing within her.

All along the way, we are uncovering what makes us tick, what makes us unique and *why* we are on this earth.

As for me, after more than five decades on the planet—ever closer to six, now that I think about it. In fact, I said to my wife recently, "You don't think I look sixty, do you, dear?" I was relieved when she said no, until she added, "But you used to." 😃 But seriously, I am finally enjoying the process of living life as it comes, facing the twists and turns that we all encounter, some of them not always pleasant to be sure, yet persevering and moving forward to continue discovering the champion within.

But maybe you do not have to suffer as much as I have. Indeed, I want to give you a head start so you do not have to wait that long to gain a sense of peace and confidence. It is never too late to live a life of incredible meaning and purpose. Don't you want that?

So jump on this journey with me. As you will see, this book is an interactive road map to healing your pain, conquering your demons and discovering your purpose. By the time you finish, you will see how to vanquish those "demons" I call "soul thieves" and create significant breakthroughs in all aspects of your life. I promise you that.

I promise that there is a new confidence that is going to come into your life through this healing and discovery process. This is exactly the weapon you need to deal with the anxious, stress-filled world that is thrown at us daily.

Let's turn pain to power. Let's uncover the treasure and true worth that our Creator has placed inside each of us. And let's unleash the grace that God has given us to make our lives, families and world a better place.

I have often said, *The best thing you can do for this world is to give it better people than yourself.* In the spirit of that cause, let's give this world a better person than who we used to be, the very best version of ourselves.

Remember: Healing and revolution from the inside out is about to turn you right side up (if you have been upside down 😊. It is going to turn your scars into stars, your test into a testimony and your pain into purpose.

We are also discovering that life is truly about perspective. *How* you see something is far more important than what it is you see. We can discover the good if we look for it—just as we can discover the bad in the same way.

So let's look for the good. Let's expect the silver lining in every cloud. Let's look for the good thing God is doing in our lives, as we trust His promise. . . .

"Follow Me," Jesus said, "and I will make you something that has never been before" (see Matthew 4:19).

Acknowledgments

I love to quote Albert Einstein (any chance I get to sound or feel a little smarter, LOL), who said, "You don't really understand something unless you can communicate it in a simple way." And yet the beliefs and feelings in our hearts are often too deep and complex to figure out alone. So *if* I have had any success at understanding the cure for soul sickness and sharing it in a simple way, it is because of the people in my life who have helped me heal my soul and, in doing so, perhaps helped themselves heal in some way as well.

I want to first and foremost thank my family, beginning with my wife, Grace. She has enthusiastically and unceasingly supported all my efforts to get this content into your hands with faith, love and prayer. The "cure" always starts at home, right? And our home was in constant need of it in order to raise five incredible children, who are by far better human beings than we could have ever imagined and far better people than me.

To Olivia, Robert, Gena, Joseph, and Roman—you are our reason. You are our dream.

I am also so grateful to all our ministry partners and especially the Life Changers International Church members, who trusted a very young man (many years ago 😊) to serve, lead and fail *forward* with, too many times to count. Your shared experience and grace have contributed so mightily to a book about the human soul.

I offer a world of thanks to my brilliant collaborator, the one and only "Glenn P," bestselling author Glenn Plaskin. His keen insight and literary skill are altogether indispensable. A true virtuoso in every way.

And my superb editor Barbara Clark, who studied, researched and graciously pored over every one of my thoughts and words to deliver you this book's best version of itself!

I also want to thank my beautiful daughter Olivia, who was instrumental in organizing the content in several parts of *Soul Cure*. As always, she is the kindest inspiration to me. And thanks to her project assistant, Jenni Birsan, who helped gather and organize many of my scattered thoughts and ideas.

A huge thanks to the best team on earth—our Life Changers staff who create such a fantastic culture of emotional health and inspire me daily with their ideas, their energy, their playful banter and love.

Special thanks to Tim Abare, chief marketing evangelist at Life Changers, who teams up daily with Branden Gurule, Robert Dickow and Joseph Dickow to inspire and shepherd our creative and marketing efforts. Tim also served as the liaison between our writing team and the publisher to make something extraordinary happen.

That leads me to Chosen Books, our outstanding publisher, who has meticulously edited and designed this book, treating it with precious faith and care, and treating me with such faith, hope and vision. My two editorial directors, Kim Bangs and Jane Campbell, were such a rare gift to us. And I am incredibly grateful that they saw something in me worth investing in and sharing with the world. And what a bonus gift to have Chosen's Deirdre Close serve as marketing director, whose enthusiasm for this project was contagious.

I'd also like to give a special thanks to Raoul Davis, the CEO of Ascendant Group Branding. Their astute marketing and publicity efforts were a great asset to us.

And finally, I want to thank the three Men I admire most—the Father, the Son and the Holy Ghost! Fortunately for you and me, they *didn't* take the last train for the coast, but instead, they made me, loved me, believed in me and stayed with me, never leaving or ever giving up on me. And They will do the same for you. Oh, what love the Father has bestowed on us that we should be called the children of God!

Now I dedicate this book to YOU, the beautiful human with a soul beyond compare. You felt inspired to open these pages today and breathe a little easier and hopefully live a little happier because of what you find in the chapters ahead. It is my honor to serve you and help remind you just how priceless you truly are.

With love,
Gregory Dickow

Introduction

A joyful heart is good medicine, but a broken spirit dries
up the bones.

Proverbs 17:22

I was visiting my oldest son the other night when I leaned over
and asked him if I could borrow a newspaper.

"Dad," he said, "it's 2022. Why would I have a newspaper?
But if you like, you can borrow my iPad."

I can tell you this: That spider never knew what hit him!

I start this book with some lighthearted humor because laughter
does good, like medicine. This is especially true in today's chaotic
world, where we definitely need a good laugh and God's healing hand.

Good news is in short supply these days, especially in headlines—
filled with fear, hate, disease and crisis.

Where is the inspiration, encouragement and hope? That ship sailed
a long time ago.

Yet the Bible says, "Eyes that focus on what is beautiful bring joy
to the heart, and hearing a good report refreshes and strengthens the
inner being" (Proverbs 15:30 TPT).

Another translation says, "Good news makes for good health" (NLT).

No wonder people are so weighed down. Our hearts are heavy,
our minds are weary as they are being flooded with bad news. This

is why the Gospel changes people's lives. It is the good news of God's love and grace.

Notice that verse talks about focus. *Whatever we are focused on will bring either joy or sorrow to our lives.*

This book is dedicated to helping you focus on what is beautiful. Why? Because what we focus on shapes the soul—the mind, the will, the emotions.

Early on in the COVID-19 crisis of 2020, when all "nonessential" businesses were completely shut down, a woman joked, "All the nail salons, hair salons and beauty salons are closed. It's about to get *ugly*!"

Well, kidding aside, life *can* get ugly. And there are a lot of ugly things in this world. That is exactly what the enemy of our soul wants us focused on. Because that is what determines the condition of the soul.

In fact, the force that drives all human emotion and interaction is *mental health*—the state of mind of my life, your life and the lives of all eight billion people on earth.

Think about it: What we say and do is a product of how we feel—the thoughts and emotions that drive us. This is the temperature of our souls. And some of us are running fevers.

Astoundingly, 450 million people worldwide currently suffer from some sort of mental disorder—46 million in the United States alone. That is 1 in 5 adults.[1]

Simply put, we all deal with emotional pain at some level. Most of us know what it is like to feel down or discouraged, depressed or anxious, obsessed or compulsive, abused or addicted—you name it.

But Better Days Are Ahead for You

This book is all about healing and freeing the soul by understanding the root causes of human suffering, emotional pain and the spiritual forces behind it all. Indeed, this book will address the dark night of the soul and offer a powerful navigational system that will dissolve fear, self-hatred, bitterness, guilt, anger and negativity.

We have all experienced these diabolical emotions, for sure. I call them *soul thieves*, which I will address in part II of this book. These are the emotions that erode your mental and physical health. And they must be dealt a deathblow.

Now is the time.

Some emotional problems and addictions may require professional intervention. But you can experience real freedom by letting God's love wash over your soul and discovering the simple steps that will unlock emotional healing and the power to change your mood on command.

As you will learn, we all have the ability to switch on positive emotions—love, hope, forgiveness, gratitude, kindness, joy, confidence and optimism. And we can choose to turn on the negative ones, too—anxiety, anger, resentment, guilt, jealousy, despair, fear and pessimism. Whichever faucet is turned on, positive or negative, that is what comes out.

Too often, as we know, we find ourselves drowning in the negative flow that pushes us downstream toward making bad decisions.

This can only lead to feeling defeated and discouraged, robbing us of our peace and God's promise of a hopeful future.

All that is going to change.

As I mentioned earlier, Proverbs 15:30 says, "Hearing a good report refreshes and strengthens the inner being" (TPT). Another translation says, "Good news gives health to the body" (NET).

And as it says in Jeremiah 30:17: "'I will restore you to health and heal your wounds,' declares the LORD" (NIV).

So buckle up and get ready, get ready, get ready for a better life to begin today. It's time to unleash God's healing and purpose for your life!

Before we go further, you might be thinking, *How is there healing power in this book? How is what I'm reading going to be different from any other self-help or faith book I've ever read? And what is Gregory Dickow's secret sauce?*

After more than 35 years of searching for a way to heal my own life and the lives of thousands of others, I have finally found the root cause of pain and pleasure, the thing that truly determines whether you feel sorrow or joy.

It is simply this: What you focus on and the way you think will determine the way you feel and the way you live.

In other words, your mindset is the single most powerful force in creating the ripple effect of shaping your emotions, your decisions, your character and your destiny. A mindset is simply an attitude that takes precedence over all other facts.

> What you focus on and the way you think will determine the way you feel and the way you live.

As I always say, "Think right, live right."

So the first step in creating a happier, more powerful life is winning the battle of the mind.

Nothing says it better than the verse "As he thinketh in his heart, so is he" (Proverbs 23:7 KJV). This means that each one of us holds the key to the conditions, good or bad, that shape our lives.

And that is why the battle for happiness is not in the heavens but in our heads. That is why some people are truly happy. It is because their minds are flooded with good news and winning thoughts, which create positive emotions and successful choices. Everything they touch eventually turns to gold, because they create and maintain positive faith-filled mindsets that will always lead to success.

Conversely, that is also why so many people are depressed—their minds are flooded with bad news and negative thoughts, which create negative emotions and lead to negative choices, all causing discouraging results.

So in this book, we will zoom in to your thought life and double-click on your soul. And as you will see (despite the statistics), the majority of us are not mentally ill. We do not need a psychiatrist or medication. What we *do* need is to change the way we think and the forces that are feeding our souls.

You are going to get real results, because happiness is not an accident. It is a pattern that you can pinpoint, create and nourish so you can get the results you deserve—a happy, victorious, peaceful, productive, loving life.

Today, my friend, we are going to heal the soul—the mind, the heart and the will—and build a new momentum, one of overwhelming gratitude and power, one of health and supernatural joy.

I can tell you that I have seen hundreds of thousands of people worldwide who have successfully transformed their lives by understanding that we have the power to change our thoughts, to *fast from wrong thinking*. This movement, which God started in my heart, then in my church, has gone viral. It is a systematic approach for healing the mind and experiencing true freedom and peace. And it never fails to deliver.

In the pages ahead, you will see that soul cure is fueled by God's beauty, a beautiful disaster called love, the discovery of your incredible worth and value, your understanding of the gift of forgiveness, and the two most powerful words on earth.

You will also learn how to battle your personal soul thieves—loneliness, depression, anger, guilt and shame. And you will discover that you can enjoy life and stop feeling bad—that you are more than your past and that your life story does not end in the chapter you are currently in. These truths will transform your thinking and fill your life until your cup is absolutely running over.

This book is all about restoring the soul, healing the storm from within, and leading you to a breakthrough transformation.

So are you ready to trade a damaged soul for a beautiful one? Soul sickness for soul health? Soul poverty for soul power?

Let's go!

PART I

SOUL
HEALTH

1

"Someone Has Stolen Our Tent!"

Look at what is obvious.

2 Corinthians 10:7 HCSB

Sherlock Holmes and Dr. Watson were on a camping trip. In the middle of the night Holmes woke up and gave Dr. Watson a nudge. "Watson," he said, "look up in the sky and tell me what you see."

"I see millions of stars, Holmes," replied Watson.

"And what do you conclude from that, Watson?"

Watson thought for a moment. "Well," he said, "astronomically, it tells me that there are millions of galaxies and potentially billions of planets. Astrologically, I observe that Saturn is in Leo. Horologically, I deduce that the time is approximately a quarter past three. Meteorologically, I suspect that we will have a beautiful day tomorrow. Theologically, I see that God is all-powerful, and we are small and insignficant. . . . Uh, what does it tell you, Holmes?"

"Watson, you idiot! Someone has stolen our tent!"

Life Lessons That We Miss

Sometimes we miss the simplest things right before our eyes.

Watson was so sophisticated and smart—with his astronomical, theological and meteorological analysis. Meanwhile, he missed the simple fact that his tent was gone.

You see? While we try to analyze our lives, examine the world, assess our situations with the highest sophistication and education, our "tents" are being robbed right from under our noses. Someone has stolen our "tents."

The answers we all need are right before our eyes, right between our ears, and smack-dab in the middle of our hearts. In other words, they are in our souls. As the soul goes, so go our lives.

This is where life is really lived—in the *soul*, the place where battles are won or lost. It is where every joy and sadness begins and where every success and failure finds its roots. The condition of your soul will determine the condition of your life. Because it determines how you think, what you feel and what you choose to do.

In other words, the soul is the source of your thoughts and your emotions and the choices you make—minute by minute, day by day.

Soul health turns into *whole* health. Soul sickness turns into *whole* sickness.

A broken soul creates a broken life, broken relationships and shattered dreams.

But all that is about to change for you. Your next days are going to be your best days. You are about to step into the life God intended for you. As Jesus put it, "I came that they may have and enjoy life, and have it in abundance (to the full, till it overflows)" (John 10:10 AMPC).

But Jesus also said, in the same verse, "The thief comes only in order to steal and kill and destroy."

The life we deserve, the one God wants most for us, has been blown away by the 24/7 news cycles, the never-ending barrage of violence and the social media overload that subjects us to constant stress and pressure. Inside and out, we are losing the calm, the safety and the security of the world as it once was. The soul of humanity is sick in many ways. Mental health—soul health—has been overtaken with soul sickness, mental anguish and people living stress-filled lives.

We all know what it is like to suffer some sort of emotional pain, don't we? (And Jesus paid for it all.) We bleed when we get injured, whether in our bodies or our hearts. It hurts.

Now multiply that hurt and consider a world filled with millions who bleed, a planet riddled with illness, fear and anxiety.

Tragically, more than one million people commit suicide each year. And more than twenty million attempt it and fail.[1] That is staggering.

There is no doubt about it: Mental "dis-ease" is an epidemic on the rise. And remember, the statistics are based upon people who admit the problem and do not include those who are suffering silently.

I hate to lay it on, but there are 20 million Americans battling addiction,[2] 10 million who are victims of domestic violence,[3] and 8 million who suffer from eating disorders[4]—not to mention the thousands of homicide and suicide victims between the ages of 5 and 24[5] and the thousands of elementary-school-age children who injure themselves—cutting their skin, burning themselves, pulling out their hair, punching themselves.[6]

Why are they doing this? It is a desperate attempt to cope with stress and relieve anxiety, loneliness and anger. In other words, they are in severe emotional pain and attempting to numb it—or, at the opposite end of the spectrum, attempting to feel something . . . anything.

And this is nothing new or original to modern culture. Self-injury goes back two thousand years. Look at Mark 5:5: "And always, night and day, he was in the mountains, and in the tombs, crying, and cutting himself with stones" (KJV).

These emotional epidemics are proof that the heart of humanity has been overtaken by soul sickness and all the misery it creates.

This means that the happy life God wants for us is under assault by an enemy that has been targeting us all our lives, as if an infrared laser beam were aimed right at the core of our beings.

To sum it up: Whether our pain is physical or emotional, whether it is heart disease or heartbreak, strokes or struggles, cancer or condemnation, people are in pain. It is part of the human condition.

No wonder Jesus came to heal. He knew that sickness, trauma and disease were crippling families, economies and destinies.

A Dark Night of the Soul

Have you ever experienced a dark night of the soul—a time when you felt desperately sad, discouraged or afraid?

Before I go any further, let me tell you that there is no shame in experiencing a dark night, dark week, dark month, dark year or dark life. Jesus gets it. He felt everything you have ever felt, and He is here now—to hear you, heal you and carry you through to the other side.

"And He took with Him Peter and James and John, and began to be struck with terror and amazement and deeply troubled and depressed. And He said to them, My soul is exceedingly sad . . . so that it almost kills Me!" (Mark 14:33–34 AMPC).

Notice that although Jesus felt everything we have ever felt, He never sinned. So it is not a sin to go through emotional pain. And this is big: *It is nothing to feel shame about.* Instead, let me encourage you to treat it as a signal that you are ready for a breakthrough; Light is coming. The hope you have lacked is going to be revived.

We all know what it is like to experience a dark moment—a moment when you are broken by some loss, failure or long-forgotten emotional wound. That is when so many of us experience disappointment or even trauma. And those toxic memories and emotions stick with us and drag us down, targeting our vulnerable souls. It is as if a trap is set, damaging our enjoyment of the present and our prospects for the future.

I sure have had my share of dark moments. I have experienced a roller coaster of emotions, including intense anxiety, anger, depression and fear, all dating back to my youth. So you may ask, *How can this guy have an answer for me? And how does he know so much about pain?*

Well, as Clubber Lang (played by Mr. T) said in *Rocky III*, when asked for his prediction for his upcoming match with Rocky. "Prediction?" he rhetorically asked. "Pain!" he answered.

The "prediction" of every day in my early years was *pain*. I just knew and expected something bad to happen every day.

Contrast that by asking my prediction for my tomorrow and every day to follow. My answer is "Glory!" I am expecting something good, something great, something *glorious* to happen in my life today. And every day. And you can too.

But at the time, my dark moments got even darker after one of my closest friends in high school, Randy, unexpectedly and tragically committed suicide just as we were entering our junior year. I can picture his young face even now, over forty years later. I can see his smile and I can see his pain.

> There is no shame in experiencing a dark night, dark week, dark month, dark year or dark life. Jesus gets it. He felt everything you have ever felt.

I was already feeling lonely and unsure of myself in those early years of life, and that moment spun me further into darkness. I had never felt God's unconditional love. I was a loner, alienated and depressed. By sixteen, I was hooked on alcohol and drugs. It was a dark night of despair.

I was already experiencing some form of depression at a young age. At the time, I had no sense of my worth or value.

Have you ever felt that way? It happens when we derive our value from the way we look or perform—and the way others see us.

Yet simultaneously somehow, Randy's death and, more accurately, his life left an indelibly profound mark on me. It awakened a desperate yearning in me to find answers from God and to find my purpose in life.

It would be some years later before I would truly understand and step into my life purpose. But it may never have happened had it not been for the friendship I found in Randy and the impact his sudden death had on me. So in a very real and deep way, I carry the memory of this young man in my soul, and his memory sometimes carries me.

In fact, my soul was in such a dark, lonely place that had God not intervened in my life, there is no telling what I might have become. Too shy and insecure to reach out for help, I turned my emotions inward. I often wonder what would have happened if I had turned my self-hatred outward.

We all know of lone wolves who act out their sorrow and rage.

All this violence unleashed in twisted minds, causing torment, sickness, heartache, murder, such unimaginable pain.

But just as God interrupted the dark night of my soul, He can interrupt yours, too.

The Bible says that we were all dead in our sins, controlled by the darkness, by the darkest version of ourselves (see Ephesians 2:3). "But God, being rich in mercy, because of His great love with which He loved us, even when we were dead in our transgressions, made us alive together with Christ (by grace you have been saved)" (verses 4–5 NASB 1995).

Do you see God as the "interrupter" here? In the middle of the fear, the loneliness, the sin, the pain—the darkness—there is a "but God" moment when He crashes through our pain, crashes through the darkness and brings the light of His healing and delivering hand. Healing comes to the soul through the power of connection. Our connection with God is our connection to healing—spirit, soul and body.

You see, my "but God" moment was happening.

As a teenager, I had very few friends, and now with Randy gone, I had even fewer, and I felt empty inside. I was traumatized by tragedy, which compounded the void I felt from the absence of a real attachment to God. I felt so depressed at times that I, too, like Randy and many others, thought of suicide. I was in a battle for my soul.

Then one night during those painful days, a young co-worker of mine busted through my solitary confinement. "Hey, man, wanna come to Bible study with me?" Rich asked.

This was my "but God" moment. There I was, on my way to another night of drugs and alcohol to dull my pain, and God interrupted me through this young man. The details of that chapter of my life I will save for another time, but that Bible study was my first encounter with God's love in my life. That Bible study was the first ray of light for my dark, lonely soul.

Psalm 119:130 says, "The entrance of Your words gives light" (NKJV).

At that Bible study, I invited Jesus Christ into my life as my Savior. That night I was born again. Light came bursting through. That was the moment when Jesus began the progressive miracle of healing my soul. He said, "Behold, I stand at the door and knock; if anyone hears My voice and opens the door, I will come in to him and will dine with him, and he with Me" (Revelation 3:20).

> "Behold, I stand at the door and knock; if anyone hears My voice and opens the door, I will come in to him and will dine with him, and he with Me."

That night, Jesus started "dining" with me—loving me, healing me. I had no concept of the journey that would begin that day. I would not only find a Savior, but I would also finally find my best Friend, Jesus, the one who sticks closer than a brother. There has not been a dull moment since. I was overcome by the love of God shown by some kind people who graciously and cheerfully welcomed a potential lone wolf into the family of God that night.

How ironic that, years later, I myself would become a pastor, leading others to the true Shepherd of their soul, the true Soul Mate that everyone longs to meet one day.

But I always fondly think back on that night, often with tears, remembering when the Light of the world, entering my lonely soul, destroyed the power of darkness, and God's love broke through. All because someone was willing to look past my walls and give me hope for the very first time.

This only proves that reaching out to a loner—a person at work, at school, in your neighborhood or in your family—can make a real difference.

We have to look around and realize that every one of us has influence in the lives of the people we come in contact with. A person may be in great emotional pain, but we can help him or her in the simplest of ways. It may be that nobody else will reach out to them—but you.

Go hit that person up with some good old-fashioned kindness and love. Kindness is never wrong. Maybe it is just a smile, or asking someone how their day is going or giving him a "Hey, man, it's gonna be all right. Let me pray for you." This is one of the simplest ways God brings healing to and through our souls.

Do not be afraid to connect. Love never fails. And love will break down barriers and drive the fear out of people's lives, including yours. I wish I had known then what I know now. Perhaps God could have used me to interrupt the enemy's plan that took the life of my dear friend. Yet somehow God used his death to interrupt the enemy's plan for me.

Fast-forward: Having now worked with hundreds of thousands of people over many decades, having preached thousands of times, I offer you the answer to the most universal prayer of all—our very real and human longing for happiness.

Know this: First and foremost, Jesus wants you well. He wants you full of joy. And he wants you happy.

As the psalmist wrote, "Happy are the people who are in such a state; happy are the people whose God is the LORD!" (Psalm 144:15 NKJV).

There is no higher or deeper desire in the heart of humankind than happiness. It is the single most popular pursuit, one that drives every decision and action in our lives.

The tragedy of this search is not that we cannot find happiness but that we search for it in the wrong places.

The great scientist and philosopher Blaise Pascal said, "All men seek happiness. . . . This is the motive of every action of every man, including those who go and hang themselves."[7]

In an effort to feel better, we turn to the familiar vices we know all too well—whether it's approval or alcohol; donuts or dates, social media or shopping till we're dropping—all to numb ourselves and escape. (Well, shopping is never wrong, is it?! Ha!)

Why? Because we are trying to escape the *pain*—anxiety, worry, loneliness and fear. So we settle for a temporary fix, a distraction, a quick high to take away the hurt.

But in this book, we find a more healthy, more long-lasting solution, a gateway to soul power. And that power begins with what we focus our attention on.

DECIDE AND DECLARE

◈ The light of God's healing and freedom floods my entire being.

◈ I expect God's pure light to crash through the dark and painful places of my soul.

◈ I set the course of my life with my words.

◈ I will live an abundant, happy, healthy life all my days.

NOW PRAY THIS WITH ME

Beginning today, I invite You, God, to heal me everywhere I'm hurting—spirit, soul and body. I invite You to interrupt my fears, anxieties, loneliness and pain. Let Your pure light crash through the dark and painful places of my soul. Thank You for hearing me, healing me and carrying me through to the other side. Thank You for giving me a life of abundance, happiness and health to the fullest, until it overflows. In Jesus' name, Amen.

2

Feed Your Soul Beauty

The Beauty of Jesus

Now there was leaning on Jesus' bosom one of His disciples, whom Jesus loved.

John 13:23 NKJV

*L*ord, love me!"

This is the heart cry of John the apostle, whom we find leaning on the bosom of Jesus at the Last Supper in John 13:23. This love, which comes from our beautiful Savior, is the secret to all that ails humankind. It finds what is lost, fills what is empty, fixes what is broken and frees what is bound.

Before we go any further, I want you to know that the purpose of this chapter is to serve as our North Star.

There is much pain in the world, as we know. But let's recall the verse I shared in the introduction: "Eyes that focus on what is *beautiful* bring joy to the heart, and hearing a good report refreshes and strengthens the inner being" (Proverbs 15:30 TPT, emphasis added).

We all need joy for our hearts and strength for our inner beings. And that is why this book is dedicated to helping you focus on what is truly beautiful—because what we focus on shapes our souls.

Feed the soul beauty, and it will heal itself.

I believe that every bit of healing you need for your heart, your soul, your mind and your emotions—and every bit of healing needed in the world at large—starts with focusing on what is truly beautiful. And Jesus is the most beautiful thing in the universe. When you begin to know Him as He wants to be known, the way He truly is, there will be no stopping the goodness. The peace. The joy.

> Jesus is the most beautiful thing in the universe.

We live in such a beautiful world—yet we have been conditioned to view life through a negative lens and feed our soul everything except beauty. The news feeds us so much of what is dark, ugly and destructive. But I pray that the cycle stops—that we start viewing life through the lens of God's beauty. Most of us see His beauty daily but do not recognize it or make the connection. So our minds remain on the negative as the norm, and our emotions take on that mindset.

We *must* feed our souls beauty. And our souls will begin to heal.

In one of the most well-known verses of Scripture, for example, Jesus gives us the cure for anxiety: "Therefore I tell you, stop being worried or anxious (perpetually uneasy, distracted) about your life" (Matthew 6:25 AMP).

Most people miss the cure. He goes on to say in verse 26, "Look at the birds of the air" (AMP).

Yes, He wants us to see that our Father feeds them, but more importantly, I believe, He wants us to see the beauty of creation.

He goes on to say, "Look at the lilies of the field and how they grow. They don't work or make their clothing" (verse 28 NLT).

Again, Jesus gives us the secret to mastering our emotions (in this case, worry and anxiety) by saying that it is all about what we are looking at.

Beauty is a signpost from and to our Creator. *Beauty brings people to Jesus*: The beautiful Christ invites us to share in His light, His life and His love—to become flooded with His unequaled goodness, His matchless wisdom, His loving presence, His healing hands. One glimpse of His brilliance can reshape our entire existence.

The multitudes said, "Lord, feed me." They were aware of their hunger.

The disciples said, "Lord, lead me." They were aware of their need for direction.

But John said, "Lord, love me." He was aware of God's beauty.

What is it that John saw? What is it that drew him to Jesus' bosom?

No angry, judgmental God would draw someone to His bosom. No punisher. No disciplinarian. No abuser, hurter, hater or indifferent God would elicit such warmth and devotion.

Sadly, so many Christians grew up with a checklist—rules and demands that must be met in order for a person to be acceptable to God. Many people reading right now may have been raised with the idea that God is a dictator, just waiting for us to step out of line so he can put us in our places.

I heard all these things about God before I discovered Him as Most Beautiful.

A wrong concept of God is the greatest problem in the world today. Because it repels people. Failure to understand how truly beautiful He is keeps us distant and cold toward a God we cannot feel or adore.

My hope in this chapter is that you will catch a glimpse of how beautiful Jesus truly is. Because when you do, it will change the trajectory of your life and send you on collision course with true happiness. One glimpse of this Beautiful Savior, and the torrents in your restless soul will cease, the loneliness will fade, the pain will subside.

A true knowledge of Jesus is every human's greatest need and our greatest happiness. To be mistaken about Him is the most tragic error of all.

The devil is trying to hijack and distort the true image of Jesus, trying to paint a wrong picture of Him. Since the beginning of creation, the enemy of our souls has been trying to vandalize the true picture of God, the goodness of God and the beauty of God. Why? Because he knows that once you discover the real Jesus, your soul can be healed of every brokenness and pain it has ever endured.

What if someone broke into the Gallery of the Academy of Florence to spray-paint graffiti on Michelangelo's *David*? Or what if someone broke into the Louvre to paint a mustache and beard on Leonardo da Vinci's *Mona Lisa*? The pure beauty of these masterpieces would be vandalized—their images distorted. Their value destroyed. They would not mean as much to us.

So, too, the devil, in the middle of the dark night of the Dark Ages, somehow managed to vandalize our image of Jesus and our concept of God in order to paint Him as an angry, distant deity.

Never once in my first twenty or thirty or even forty years on earth did I hear anyone say that God is ultimate beauty. Never once did I hear the idea that everything precious, true, beautiful and good is found in Him. Never once did anyone tell me that He is altogether lovely. No wonder I searched for meaning and fulfillment in everything *except* Him.

But when I began to discover how stunningly beautiful He truly is, I started to enjoy knowing, loving and worshiping Him as my most beautiful Savior and friend rather than "serving" Him as Lord and master. I could lose everything today, but as long as I have Him, I have everything.

This is the secret to a satisfied and healthy soul.

The Gospel is not a set of rules to live by. It is a mosaic of Jesus' beauty.

The Gospel is not a set of rules to live by. It is a mosaic of Jesus' beauty. The Bible is the greatest work of art because it paints, in story form, the beauty of Jesus throughout its pages.

Preaching the Bible as a set of laws and rules will never change a heart or a life. That is not God's way. The Bible is a map pointing to and leading to the the greatest treasure of all time—Jesus and His matchless love. Everything that makes Him beautiful is woven throughout the fabric of Scripture.

Consider the story of two sisters who invited Jesus to their home. You know what is so amazing about that? He accepted the invitation— just as He promised He would to whoever invites Him in.

When Jesus arrived at Martha and Mary's home, one of them was bothered; the other was free. One was in a tizzy; the other was in love. One was at her wits' end; the other was at peace (Luke 10:38–42).

What made the difference?

Focus.

Mary was focused on Jesus' beauty, sitting at His feet, listening to the pearls of love and wisdom coming from her Savior. Martha was focused on what had to be done; what had to be cleaned; what had to be prepared for her Lord. Their entire emotional lives were based on one thing: what they were focused on.[1]

And consider Acts 8:26–38. Two thousand years ago, an African man who knew nothing about Jesus was sitting in a chariot on the road between Jerusalem and Gaza. At that time, God directed an evangelist named Philip to overtake the chariot.

> So Philip ran to him, and heard him reading the prophet Isaiah, and said, "Do you understand what you are reading?"
> And he said, "How can I, unless someone guides me?" And he asked Philip to come up and sit with him. The place in the Scripture which he read was this:
>
> > "He was led as a sheep to the slaughter;
> > And as a lamb before its shearer is silent,
> > So He opened not His mouth.
> > In His humiliation His justice was taken away,
> > And who will declare His generation?
> > For His life is taken from the earth."
>
> So the eunuch answered Philip and said, "I ask you, of whom does the prophet say this, of himself or of some other man?"

Then Philip opened his mouth, and beginning at this Scripture, preached Jesus to him. (verses 30–35 NKJV)

Notice that Philip did not preach commandments. He did not see Scripture as a book of rules and demands. He found a description of Jesus exactly where the Ethiopian eunuch was reading and preached Jesus to him. Had Philip opened the book to another passage, he would have found the same thing: Jesus.

> Christianity is not a religion. It is a relationship with God.

You see, Christianity is not a religion; it is a relationship with God. And the Bible is not a book of rules. It's a mosaic of Jesus Christ's beauty. That is why religious people find God tolerable and useful, but people who have been touched by His love find Him beautiful and indispensable.

A Definition of Beauty

Beauty is penultimate—second to the last in a sequence of things.

Beauty is amazing. It makes us laugh and cry, come alive and be joyful. But beauty was never intended to be the ultimate object of our attention.

The sunset, the symphony, the work of art, they are not supreme. They are not the last word on beauty. They are not ends in themselves. Beautiful things are a means to an end. Beauty is a signpost, a pointer, a foretaste of the ultimate—namely, Jesus.

All the beauty of this world—the galaxies, the oceans; all the symphonies, music, poetry ever written; every beautiful human who ever lived; every painting, forest, star, animal—all these are finite. All this is created beauty—created by the infinite one, who is beauty itself.

In fact, if you added all created beauty together, it would still be less than a speck compared to the unending, limitless loveliness of Jesus Christ.

How beautiful is Jesus? I heard it said . . .

"He is altogether lovely" (Song of Solomon 5:16 KJV). I heard it said . . .

1. *How beautiful are His hands* as He heals the sick, cleanses the lepers, multiplies bread to feed the multitudes. Then was pierced for our salvation and healing.
2. *How beautiful are His feet,* pierced for our sins, after years of walking mile after mile bringing healing power, love, and salvation to whosoever believes.
3. *How beautiful is His embrace,* as children go running toward Him to be caught up in His arms and as He lays His hands on each of them, blessing them with His sacred and tender touch.
4. *How beautiful is His prayer* when He prays in John 17:23, that the world would know that the Father sent Him, and that the Father loves us as He loves Jesus.
5. *How beautiful is His humility* when in John 13:3, Jesus knew that the Father had put all things under His power. Upon knowing this, Jesus didn't take a bow, a throne, or a victory lap. He took a towel and washed His disciples' feet.
6. *How beautiful is His handwriting* as He stoops down in front of the woman caught in adultery and writes in the dirt the words that set her free.
7. *How beautiful is His love* in John 11:3–5, when they said, "Jesus, the one whom You love is sick." Jesus loved Martha, Mary, and Lazarus. . . .
8. *How beautiful are His tears* when in John 11:33, He sees Mary weeping and is moved deeply—in verse 35, "Jesus wept."
9. *How beautiful is His brow,* as it is pierced through by a crown of thorns. The greatest King and the most brilliant mind is bloodied by a punishing crown He wore for you and me.
10. *How beautiful are His eyes* that looked at the thief on the cross as His own friend, without condemnation, promising him, "Today you shall be with Me in Paradise." (Luke 23:43)[2]

Anyone who thinks heaven will be boring simply has no true knowledge of Jesus' infinite beauty.

You see, religion has robbed us of the pure beauty and true concept of God. The author of Hebrews 1:3 said that Jesus is "the radiance of [God's] glory and the exact representation of His nature."

Or, in another translation, Jesus "perfectly mirrors God, and is stamped with God's nature" (MSG).

John only saw a glimpse of His beauty and was drawn immediately to His bosom.

No wonder David said, "I'm asking GOD for one thing, only one thing: To live with him in his house my whole life long. I'll contemplate his beauty; I'll study at his feet" (Psalm 27:4 MSG).

"No wonder Mary sat at His feet after experiencing His forgiveness and His defense of her soul. 'Leave her alone!' He said when the Pharisees, blinded by their self-righteousness, wanted her dead (Mark 14:6)."[3]

John, David and Mary all had one thing in common: They caught a glimpse of Jesus' beauty, and they were drawn to Him as a magnet is to steel.

The moment we awaken in heaven, we will catch our first glimpse of the face of Jesus Christ. We will be awestruck, enraptured forever. Whatever we have considered beautiful before will seem dead compared with the stunning loveliness of Jesus' face.

As soon as we see that look of perfect, holy love, we will drop to our knees in utter amazement as love and gratitude create in us a flood of praise and worship that will last throughout eternity.

Jesus is in every book of the Bible, described or foretold in some way, just as He is in every area and season of your life, even those you never realized.

He is in your past, to assure you it is washed away. He is in your future, to assure you it will be okay. He is in your pain, to heal you where you are hurting. He is in your song, giving you reason to sing. He is in your weakness, to bring you strength. He is in your loneliness, to be your comfort.

Jesus is both beauty and the author of beauty. His stories are full of defining moments that prove His beauty and glory. He tells us stories of celebration. A master hosts a banquet and invites the forsaken and forgotten. A father throws a party for a prodigal son's return. A shepherd sends angels dancing at the rescue of one lost sheep.

Jesus turns ashes into beauty, water into wine, sickness into health, sinners into saints, slaves into free men, prostitutes into preachers. And He does all this in his spare time, as He prepares to empty Himself on the cross, reuniting us with the source of all that is good and beautiful—our heavenly Father.

> Jesus is both beauty and the author of beauty.

More than one thousand years ago, Vladimir the Great, grand prince of Kiev, was looking for a new faith that would unify his people. He sent out ambassadors to explore and discover the great faiths of the world. They came back and described faiths that were reverent and philosophical but had no gladness. But then they described the greatest of all. A faith that was transcendent, a faith whose adherents led them to Christ-centered Constantinople.

After they had attended services in the great Hagia Sophia, a Byzantine Christian church at the time, the ambassadors told their master: "We know not whether we were in Heaven or on earth, for surely there is no such splendor or beauty anywhere upon earth. We cannot describe it to you; only we know that God dwells there among men, and that their service surpasses the worship of all other places. For we cannot forget that beauty."[4]

They could not forget that beauty.

Everything that God creates, and every person who has been touched by His love, emanates beauty and an aura that cannot be denied.

A Rose of Sharon

"I am the rose of Sharon."
Song of Solomon 2:1

42

Jesus is not simply a rose. He is the rose of Sharon.

If you pull this rose apart, petal by petal, and place the petals in a jar, you will find that each retains its fragrant aroma, filling the house with perfume.

Jesus is that fragrant aroma, an aroma that satisfies both the most and the least sophisticated senses.

In John 10:11, Jesus described himself with the words "I am the good shepherd," or, in Greek, "Eimi kalos poimēn." The Greek word *kalos* means "beautiful"; according to Strong's *Exhaustive Concordance of the Bible*, its formal definition is "attractively good; good that inspires (motivates) others to embrace what is lovely (beautiful, praiseworthy); i.e., well done so as to be winsome (appealing)."

Philippians 4:8 tells us to fix our thoughts on "what is true, and honorable, and right, and pure, and lovely, and admirable. Think about things that are excellent and worthy of praise" (NLT).

What is the one thing that can embody all this? Actually, there is no one thing, but there is one person: Jesus.

So, for example, if you are trying to get your mind off your problems, it is easier than you think. It is not about condemning yourself, criticizing yourself or berating yourself for your sins and mistakes.

It is about seeing something beautiful that captivates your attention. Jesus is that something.

As it says in Song of Solomon 5:16, "His mouth is most sweet: yea, he is altogether lovely. This is my beloved, and this is my friend" (KJV).

That verse was included in the lyrics to a 1931 hymn:

> Altogether lovely,
> He is altogether lovely,
> And the fairest of ten thousand,
> This wonderful Friend divine;
> He gave Himself to save me,
> Now He lives in heav'n to keep me,
> He is altogether lovely,
> Is this wonderful Savior of mine.[5]

How could anyone reject this Savior of the world? They have not made the connection between Jesus and His beauty. But in the words of John Calvin, God gave us beauty "for delight and good cheer."

Artists help us see this beauty. They bring us to the understanding that all beauty is created by someone. An artist should understand most the artistry of God. We are God's art. We are God's poem, created to display His beauty and goodness.

You are God's work of art.

"We have become his poetry, a re-created people that will fulfill the destiny he has given each of us, for we are joined to Jesus, the Anointed One. Even before we were born, God planned in advance our destiny and the good works we would do to fulfill it!" (Ephesians 2:10 TPT).

You are God's work of art, created to carry on that beauty. This is why you must truly understand your own value. I will show you how in the next chapter.

DECIDE AND DECLARE

- ◈ Today I decide to focus on what is beautiful and good.
- ◈ I reject distorted views of God that produce fear and anxiety.
- ◈ I open my soul to the ultimate beauty, goodness and grace of God.
- ◈ I choose to rebuild the emotional foundation of my life upon the goodness of God.

NOW PRAY THIS WITH ME

Thank You, God, for creating beauty to fill my soul and bringing joy to my heart. I invite You to refresh and strengthen my entire being, from the inside out. I choose to sit at Your feet, Jesus, and

allow you to feed my soul with Your beauty and all that You cre-
ated. Flood my soul with Your goodness and grace all the days of
my life. I invite You, Jesus, to turn the ashes of my life into beauty,
the water of my life into wine and the sickness in my life into heal-
ing, Amen.

3

Your Beautiful Immortal Soul

Beautiful thoughts build a beautiful soul. There's always
something beautiful to be experienced wherever you are.

Wayne Dyer

What is the human soul? And why is it so powerful, serving as the title of this book?

The soul is eternal and beautifully ageless. It is the immortal part of every human being, the home of our personality and emotions. (Different from our "spirit," which is born again when we receive Jesus Christ as our Savior).

As I always say, the soul, simply put, is your mind to think, your heart to feel and your will to decide. It is the very deepest part of our humanity, the source of all talent and treasure. Within it grow our intellect, our emotions, our values and our perspectives on life. The soul drives all commerce, art and culture.

In short, your soul is your most valuable possession, with the fingerprint of God upon it, including your precious DNA.

I can tell you that soul power ripples outward in all directions, affecting everything—physical health, emotional well-being, relationships, families, work and destiny.

It is where every life battle is won or lost. It is where joy and sadness begin. It is where success and failure find their origins. So as the soul goes, so goes your entire life.

At birth, the soul is untouched and innocent.

But then it is damaged and corrupted by the hurts we have suffered, the mistakes we have made and the inherent fallen nature we inherited from Adam and Eve. Still, God has a remedy for that. He gives us new life spiritually when we are born again. He begins a process of healing by renewing our minds and transforming our thinking. As the great psalm declares, "He restores my soul" (23:3).

That is what this book is all about. Healing. Restoring. Enjoying who you are and what God made you for!

After Jesus rose from the dead, He met with His disciples and gave them three things they would later find indispensable.

> Then the same day at evening, being the first of the sabbaths, when the doors were shut where the disciples were assembled for fear of the Jews, Jesus came and stood in the midst and said to them, . . . Peace be unto you; as my Father has sent me, even so send I you. And when he had said this, he breathed on them and said unto them, Receive ye the Holy Spirit.
>
> John 20:19, 21–22 JUB

Notice the three gifts He gave:

- *Peace* ("Peace be unto you").
- *Purpose* ("As my Father has sent me, even so send I you").
- *Power* ("He breathed on them and said unto them, Receive ye the Holy Spirit").

God gives you these same three gifts to ready your soul for the world you face each and every day. He wants to bring you to a place of peace, a place of purpose (where you can discover your unique giftedness and treasure and share it with others) and a place of power (where you can handle anything that comes your way, where you can conquer life rather than be conquered by it). In short, He wants to make you whole inside.

Let's start with *peace*, because so many people are trying to find it. The world is filled with worry and anxiety, fear and uncertainty. So the first thing He wants your soul to experience is a true sense of calm. Jesus slept in a boat in the middle of a storm (see Mark 4:35–39). How could He do that? Because He carried His peace inside. And so can you. In fact, when His disciples fearfully woke him up, He rose up and spoke to the storm: "Peace, be still," and then it says, "there was a great calm" (verse 39 KJV). The only one who can speak to the storm is the one who is not afraid of it. And there is great calm when you know that God is with you. He will never leave you or forsake you. As you awaken to the fact that God's love for you is unconditional, peace will flow in your life, like a river.

The second thing God empowers our souls with is *purpose*—a reason to live. Your purpose starts with knowing that you are loved (which we will dig into in the next chapter) and that you were God's idea, conceived by God's love and made priceless by Him. Then it extends to discovering your true purpose on earth—the thing you were destined to do.

Without a sense of destiny and purpose, it is easy to feel lost. In fact, I believe the most depressing thing in life is to live without purpose. People only lose their way when they lose their "why." Your why is the reason for your existence.

At this moment in time, you might be weary or angry if you are not doing what you were born to do, but when you step into your God-given destiny—that gift you can give others—you will be amazed at how vibrant you feel. And it starts in your soul.

In fact, when you understand why you were born, you can handle whatever comes your way. You stop running from your past, from your pain and from your mistakes. You stop being haunted by your shortcomings. You stop beating yourself up about what you feel ashamed about or the things you did not do right. Your fears, anxieties and insecurities are finally lifted from your shoulders.

Look at this amazing verse: "They seldom reflect on the days of their life, because God keeps them occupied with gladness of heart." (Ecclesiastes 5:20 NIV).

We live in regret when we are not occupied with gladness. God wants to occupy *your* life with gladness—to fill the holes in your heart with His peace, power and purpose.

I love the way it is written in the New Living Translation: "God keeps such people so busy enjoying life that they take no time to brood over the past."

This is what will happen to *you*. God is gonna keep you so busy enjoying life that you will not live in the past—not in regret, shame or failure.

His purpose gives you stability and perspective, especially when your emotions fluctuate. After all, they are e-*motions*, always pushing you in one direction or another. This internal motion tries to sway you and force you to make bad decisions.

For example, anger is an emotion that can put into motion the desire to hurt somebody. Fear gets you to run away from something. And anxiety moves you to panic about something.

Depression moves people to take a drug or drink too much or go on eating binges. But when you understand your true purpose, it will fortify your faith and power you through negative emotions. Stop for a second and rejoice: Your emotions are trying to take you one way, but you have the freedom to go a different way. You do not have to give those emotions the power to control your choices. When you know this, you stop being an emotionally ruled person. Emotions are like the wind, blowing against you, yet you can still walk in the direction *you* choose to go.

In short: Purpose gives perspective to your pain and powers you through it. Without it, your pain can paralyze you.

That is why God also gives you *power*, a resilience and strength built into your soul. As it says in John 20:22, "He breathed on them, and said to them, 'Receive the Holy Spirit'" (NKJV). Why is it so important that we have the Holy Spirit's power?

Because every negative emotion that stirs our lives comes from a sense of powerlessness.

For example, if we do not feel we have the power to change something, it can cause depression. If we do not feel we have the power to reconcile a relationship, it can cause anger and bitterness. If we do not feel we have the power to get ahead, it can turn into jealousy.

The Holy Spirit calms our emotions, freeing us from a sense of powerlessness. "You shall receive power when the Holy Spirit comes upon you" (Acts 1:8 MEV).

The Holy Spirit is the very presence and power of God in our lives. When God said, "I will never leave you or forsake you" (Hebrews 13:5 HCSB), He had the Holy Spirit in mind. The Holy Spirit is God *with* us, God *in* us, God *for* us and God *through* us.

The Spirit of God and the Word of God make your soul as strong as steel, both durable and resilient. You have bounce-back power, the ability to rebound from adversity and devastation and carry yourself forward, no matter what the challenge.

As it says in Proverbs 24:16: "For a righteous man falls seven times and rises again." The word *righteous* in this context also means "approved." In other words, God approves of you because He made you and gave you His Son.

There is something very powerful about feeling approved. It gives you courage. It frees you from other people's opinions of you. It protects you from condemnation and discouragement of heart. The apostle Paul calls it "the breastplate of God's approval" (Ephesians 6:14 TLB).

So like a boxer who has been knocked down but gets up again, your soul is durable and resilient, tough and determined. Believe that about yourself. You have what it takes to endure heartbreak and pain, indescribable loss, discouragement and disappointment.

In short, the designer of your soul (God) gives it its value; the durability of your soul gives you the strength to persevere through anything; and the demand for your soul makes it priceless.

Did you know your soul is in high demand? That's right. There is a battle over your soul because it is so valuable. God wants to occupy it and flood it with His love and power. And the devil wants it, too, in order to keep it damaged, broken and sick.

Jesus said to Peter, "Behold, Satan demanded to have you, that he might sift you like wheat" (Luke 22:31 RSV). Jesus, however, went on to say, "But I have prayed for you . . . that your faith will not fail" (Luke 22:32 GWT).

Sometimes our faith wavers, but Jesus will not let it fail.

And He will not fail you.

Despite the promise of the three *ps*—peace, purpose and power—many of us still struggle with feelings of discouragement and defeat. We may also feel flawed and defective, unaware of our true worth. You read some of my story in an earlier chapter. And it was not pretty.

So know this: When we encounter a challenge in life, we sometimes quit before the miracle happens. Why? Because we are trying to escape our pain. So we attempt to live crisis-free lives, insulated in our self-protective bubbles of denial, doing anything we can to avoid the pain.

But pain is actually a signal that you are being sent upward to God, who will lead you into barrier-breaking territory. A crisis is not a defeat. Jesus said, "In the world you have tribulation, but take courage; I have overcome the world" (John 16:33).

> "In the world you have tribulation, but take courage; I have overcome the world."

What a powerful promise. He has overcome your pain and given you the victory. That is why He tells us we are "more than conquerors" (Romans 8:37 MEV). But how can we be *more* than conquerors? Isn't being a conqueror sufficient? Well, what makes you more than a conqueror is that you do not have to do any conquering. Jesus did all the conquering, but you get to walk in the victory! That is why you are more than a conqueror.

So rejoice in your trials, because they will lose their power when you stare them down with confident expectation of God's goodness in your life. Ultimately, they will only strengthen you. Remember, no matter how many times you failed or have fallen, no matter how many times you have denied God, He will not deny you.

Remember this, too: You have a true mission on earth. When you understand that, you can survive anything. Take a moment before going any further and ask God to reveal your God-given purpose.

Pray something like this: "Heavenly Father, I thank You that I was your idea. You knew me and gave me my destiny from the foundation of the world. So I am asking You to reveal to me Your purpose for my life and grant me the wisdom to understand and fulfill it, Amen."

Now live with expectation.

It will unfold step by step. Read the next chapter. Reach out to the next person. Pray the next prayer. Forgive the next offender.

Even when your soul feels weary or numb, keep on taking that one next step. That is God's promise: No matter how many times you fail or blow it or fall, He will not deny you. You will always get back up again.

Why? Because God's love is not at war with your behavior—your mistakes and failures. His love is set on you. It is unconditional. He will not abandon or condemn you. Instead, He looks at you with acceptance and forgiveness. And when you know this kind of love, you stop looking for love in the wrong places—in other people's opinions or approval.

Your heavenly Father's love elevates you to a place where you can dream big dreams—where you can live with purpose, unafraid. As it says in Ephesians 1:4: "Even before the world was made, God chose us for Himself" (NLV).

I promise you that your purpose, discovered in your soul, will power you through a damaged life—through pain, regrets and mistakes—and help you create a new one.

And with another breath, you have hope. And your soul can prosper once again.

DECIDE AND DECLARE

◈ My soul is eternal and precious because I was God's idea.

◈ I am being restored, strengthened and renewed by God's grace.

◈ I have God's peace, promises and power to fulfill my life purpose.

◈ Starting today I will dream big dreams with God's help.

NOW PRAY THIS WITH ME

Beginning today, I invite You, Holy Spirit, to reveal Your purpose for me, and give me the wisdom and understanding to walk in that purpose. Help me to no longer look with regret at my past, and instead fill the days of my life with joy and gladness of heart. I believe You are reviving my soul through Your grace. Thank You for giving me a healthy soul that will power me through my pain, into my purpose, launching me beyond my previous limits, Amen.

4

Get Swept Away

A Beautiful Disaster

God's not mad at you. He's mad about you!

Gregory Dickow

The year was 1992. I had just moved to Chicago a year earlier. I was minding my own business, trying to earn a living
while raising a young family and getting a fledgling Bible
study group off the ground. Then suddenly, out of nowhere, I heard a
voice whisper to my heart, *I'm not mad* at *you. I'm mad* about *you! Tell
My people that!* I knew it was the voice of God. And while my understanding of His love had a long way to go at the time—and still does—
right then something exploded inside me. My purpose in life was born.

The next day I told anyone who would listen: "God's not mad *at* you.
He's mad *about* you!" This is the cornerstone of everything I believe,
live and teach.

We are not saved by an angry God. Rather, we are rescued by a
heavenly Father who is madly in love with us. And my life's mission is
to get that message into every heart and soul I come into contact with.

54

It is what changed my life. It is what rescued me from the "religion" of rules and condemnation. It freed me from fear, inferiority and a wrong concept of God. It is what pulled me out of my emotional storm of loneliness, pain and anxiety.

From that day, I knew: I was loved and adored by God.

And when that happened to me, it was what I call a beautiful disaster. *It wrecked me.* How? It wrecked my judgmental edge. It wrecked my religion of rules. It wrecked my small vision for my life. When it hit me, it wrecked my old fears and limitations. It wrecked my old view of myself and others. It wrecked my self-criticism and insecurity. And it wrecked my despair, leveling it to the ground. It changed everything—the way I think, feel and act. It rocked my heart and soul. And it will yours as well.

As King Solomon wrote so beautifully and passionately in Song of Solomon 8:7: "Love is invincible facing danger and death. Passion laughs at the terrors of hell. The fire of love stops at nothing—it sweeps everything before it. Flood waters can't drown love, torrents of rain can't put it out" (MSG).

God's love is a beautiful disaster. When it hits you, it changes everything inside you.

Read Solomon's description more closely.

God's love is invincible. This means it is too powerful to be defeated or overcome.

God's love laughs. True joy flows from feeling truly loved.

God's love is unstoppable. It is continuous, superior to any force that would try to minimize or eliminate it. It stops at nothing, and nothing can stop it.

> God's love sweeps away everything before it.

Wow! That is what I am talking about. That is what God feels toward you.

God's love sweeps away everything before it. It sweeps away your past, your pain, your fears and your regrets.

When the love of God hits you in this way, and I am praying that it will, you will not remain the same. Brokenness will be healed.

Emptiness will be filled. Loneliness will be swallowed up. And that, my friend, is the beautiful disaster about to sweep through your life.

Let me say it again: God's love stops at nothing, and nothing can stop it.

His love sweeps away your low self-worth, your wrong beliefs, your broken desires—the addictions and compulsions that keep you from feeling whole.

As the Scripture says in Isaiah 44:22: "I have swept away your sins like a cloud" (NLT). So no longer does that cloud hang over us, blocking our view of God's love.

He storms into our lives with a vengeance—not to hurt us but to blow away what *has* been hurting us, to bring disaster to what has brought *us* disaster all our lives.

His vengeance is not against you; it is against the things that are hurting you.

He takes vengeance on our fear, our anxiety, our pain and our sickness; He takes vengeance on anything that tries to wound His beloved children—and get between you and Him.

Just as it did to me, God's love is going to "wreck" you.

When you feel it, as I first did all those years ago, it will sweep you off of your feet and take you to a place you have never been before. Feelings of inferiority will drop off like a shabby old coat that has been hanging around for far too long.

You will be clothed in something finer, wrapped up in the love of God, no longer judged by others or yourself, no longer defined by your accomplishments or failures.

His love is unbreakable—a perfect, total, unmerited gift. There is nothing you can do to gain it and nothing you can do to lose it. And it is not dependent on how you perform.

God says to us so clearly in Malachi 1:2, "I have always loved you" (NLT).

"But God," you might say, "did you love me even when I failed?"

God says, *I have always loved you!*

"Even when I sinned?"

I have always loved you.

"Even in my darkest night?"

I have always loved you!

"Even in my fits of rage?"

I have always loved you!

"Even when I had doubts and fears?"

I have always *loved you!*

There is no exception. He has *always loved you.* You are the object of His love.

You do not have to earn God's love or impress Him to get it.

We are human beings, not human doings. Just being is enough.

This means that no matter what you have done or what has been done to you, no matter who you are, you are loved—valued, accepted, chosen, blessed and treasured by God.

Let this sink in. Knowing this is the Good News, the Gospel of Jesus Christ, the heart and soul of a satisfied life.

It reminds me of the bride in Song of Solomon 2:16, who says, "My lover is mine, and I am his" (MSG). That is how God feels about you.

> No matter what you have done or what has been done to you, no matter who you are, you are loved.

Yet so often, when the soul is suffering, we start to believe that God is punishing us, that He is mad at us.

A while back, after a devastating hurricane had hit the New York region, I read a headline in the *New York Post* that summed up the distorted view of God that so many people have. It read, "GOD HATES US!" And it reminded me that so many people feel this way when something bad happens.

Such was the case with the children of Israel in Deuteronomy 1:27, when they said, "Because the LORD hates us, He has brought us out of the land of Egypt, to hand us over to the Amorites to destroy us."

That could not be further from the truth. God did not hate the children of Israel. He delivered them from countless enemies and disasters.

But their distorted view of Him shaped their beliefs and decisions, just as people's distorted views shape their minds today.

We sometimes believe that God is judging us because something goes wrong in our lives or because we feel defeated, discouraged, unworthy, unlucky or un-something else.

That is why we need to know that God loves us no matter who we are, what we do or what we go through.

He is *not* a God of wrath and judgment but one of justice and righteousness. He poured out His wrath on Jesus on the cross so He could pour out His kindness and love on *you*. I will say it again: God's not mad *at* you. He's mad *about* you! In fact, He is crazy about you.

> God's not mad at you. He's mad about you!

Jesus knew this when He heard these words coming out of heaven after being baptized by John the Baptist: "You are My beloved Son, in whom I am well pleased" (Mark 1:11 NKJV).

We need to learn to be loved—to be who God created us to be. This is the greatest source of happiness anyone can have—the assurance that we are truly loved by our heavenly Father and our Savior, Jesus.

As the Scripture says in Jeremiah 31:3–4: The Lord appeared and said, "I have loved you with an everlasting love. . . . I will build you up again. . . . You will take up your timbrels and go out to dance with the joyful" (NIV). *The Message* says it this way: "I've never quit loving you and never will. Expect love, love, and more love!"

You see, God is describing the kind of relationship He wants to have with you. There is nothing you can do to add to or subtract from His love. It is His grace that saves you (see Ephesians 2:8). And His grace is the outpouring of His love. He wants you to be sure of His love. This is what anchors your soul. This is what builds you up—what gives you something to sing and dance about, something to celebrate and something to help make you a more fruitful and successful person than you ever imagined.

Even when you fail and run from God, His arms are open wide, waiting for your return. In fact, He comes running to *you*. He chases you down. He never gives up on you. He is never angry with you. In all our seasons. In all our ups and downs. In all our failures and disappointments, nothing can separate us from His love.

What am I trying to get across? I am trying to wreck your misconception of a God who is mad at or indifferent toward you and your everyday life. It is time to dismantle the expectations of judgment and fate. And start expecting love, love and more love.

Don't you want to experience God like that? Don't you want a Christianity like that? Well, that is actually what true Christianity is. We have just been sold a distorted view of God. And I am determined to tear down those false images of our Father. His love is so full of goodness and mercy that we do not have to seek it. Why? Because His love (His goodness and mercy) will follow us and chase us down *all* the days of our life (see Psalm 23:6).

How beautifully this is illustrated in Luke 15:20–24. The Prodigal Son's father did not wait for his son to get all the way home to welcome him. As soon as he caught a glimpse of his son returning in the far off distance, he ran to him, threw his arms around him and kissed him continually. The father did not wait for an explanation. He did not wait for an apology. He did not shame him into submission.

And as soon as the son tried to earn a place back with his father, the father interrupted his son's speech that he had practiced on the way home. Just as the son was about to say, "Father, I have sinned against heaven," the father made it known that he was not going to tolerate any self-loathing, self-hating pity party. The father had a different kind of party in mind.

Before the son could get his full apology out of his mouth, his father told the servants to bring the best robe and put it on his son. He told them to get the signet ring of authority for his finger, put new sandals on his feet and kill the fatted calf. They would celebrate all night long, he said. His son was lost. Now he was home. He was dead. Now he was alive. *The Message* says at the end of verse 24, "And they began to have a wonderful time."

"They began to have a wonderful time"? Wow! Who has ever thought of that when relating to God? But that is what God wants for us. This earthly father had *that* much love for his son. How much more our heavenly Father loves us. He loves us so much more than we could ever love. Even when we fail, He is not waiting for us to grovel or beg to earn back a place with Him. He is running toward *us* with His arms open wide.

This is the kind of wonderful love He has for you. All-forgiving, overflowing, never-ending, nonjudging, uncompromising, unconditional love.

The Love Drug

In the wake of the beautiful disaster—the wreckage of God's love—precious, tangible benefits are left behind. Let's call them side effects.

In fact, research about the science of attachment has shown that love, expressed or felt, is a powerful drug that positively affects the brain and the body.

When you fall in love, the brain actively produces high levels of feel-good neurotransmitters—serotonin, dopamine and norepinephrine. These are the body's natural antidepressants, miraculous chemicals that positively influence our emotions and moods. They give us a feeling of intense pleasure and gratification, total satisfaction. It is the high of all highs, the same sensation people get when they use illicit drugs such as cocaine. But love is a natural high. And the chemicals produced in the brain in a "love state" are so powerful that they reduce the perception and sometimes even the presence of physical pain.

Wow! That is a double benefit. You feel ecstatic mentally and physically. So love is a drug without the *negative* side effects of painkillers and antidepressants.

Here is how powerfully love affects the brain: In a study done at Stanford University, researchers demonstrated that when participants viewed photos of loved ones, their brains produced notably higher levels of dopamine.

In addition, when these same participants were subjected to mild physical pain, they did not feel it. The physicians noted that *the same part of the brain* triggered by morphine and cocaine is stimulated by intense feelings of love.

This led one of the Stanford researchers to acknowledge that the way we manage pain today will be considered medieval generations from now: "We use antidepressants, antiseizure drugs, and cardiac arrhythmia drugs to treat pain in patients who don't have seizures or arrhythmias and may not even be depressed," he said.[1]

So what are many of us really suffering from? It is the absence of love.

And what is the cure? Unconditional love. This is the kind of love only God can give. And it is His pleasure to do so. We live our lives trying to experience that kind of love.

No wonder it has been proved that getting married and staying married reduces depression in both men and women. Why? Because this unconditional-love relationship reduces the anxiety and depression so often associated with social isolation and lack of connectedness.

In short, we all want and need intimacy. In fact, it is essential to our survival.

Did you know that babies who are not held, cuddled or hugged can actually stop growing? It is true. A while back, researchers had discovered that orphanages report a 30 to 40 percent infant mortality rate; babies aged zero to five just cannot receive enough stimulation in group residential care to develop to their full capability. For babies, a caress is much more than just comfort; it is essential for their well-being. Without it, the rate of illness and death is exponentially higher—so a lack of love can be a literal killer.[2]

That is how important human contact and God's love working through us can be. Deprived of it, we all suffer and can even die from it.

So whether in childhood or adulthood, we must be touched lovingly and cared for—which allows us to feel safe, secure and connected. It is the only pathway to happiness. As the great French poet and novelist

Victor Hugo wrote: "The supreme happiness in life is the assurance of being loved."[3]

And what happens in the absence of love? A lot of bad things. Consider the number of deadly mass shootings in America: According to CBS News, there were 337 of them in 2018 and 417 in 2019.[4]

These tragic massacres were caused by emotionally and mentally disturbed people, tortured souls who had a distorted view of God, which shaped their view of themselves and the world. Although each murderer had his own motives and a unique family history, there is, I believe, one common thread to this chaos: Almost all the perpetrators had some form of emotional "dis-order."

Is it possible that vast doses of love from parents, teachers or churches could have made a difference? I believe it would have, which is why I am writing this book.

As it says in 1 John 4:8: "Whoever does not love does not know God, because God is love" (NIV).

When we get hold of that love, it flows into every area of our lives. It gets into our DNA and awakens the positive emotions that each of us was meant to experience. And it cures the forces trying to defeat, depress and destroy us.

"Whoever does not love does not know God, because God is love."

So ultimately, encouraging people to feel love from God, and therefore to be able to love ourselves and others, leads to stable, supportive relationships that can potentially help people suffering from mental illness.

Some years ago, the renowned American psychiatrist Dr. Karl Menninger proved this very point in an experiment seeking the cause of patients' emotional ailments. He fervently believed that the absence of parental love accounted for many individuals' destructive urges and mental illnesses.

With that in mind, one day Dr. Menninger called in his staff and proposed an innovative plan for creating an atmosphere of loving-kindness in his treatment center. The nurses and doctors were instructed to make a mammoth effort to treat all patients lovingly and to be supportive and nurturing in all conversation. No unloving attitudes, criticism or judgments were to be displayed. At the end of six months, the average time spent by patients in the Menninger Clinic was cut in half.

How was that possible? Because love never fails. It fills the holes and gaps in our lives.

As it is written in 2 Thessalonians 2:16–17: "May our Lord Jesus Christ himself and God our Father, who loved us and by his grace gave us eternal encouragement and good hope, encourage your hearts and strengthen you in every good deed and word" (NIV).

Better Than Wine

So how good is God's love? Let me put it this way: His love is *better* than wine.

This reminds me of a story I once heard.

One day a police officer pulled over a priest for a traffic violation. The priest rolled down his window, and the officer smelled liquor on the priest's breath. Then he noticed an empty wine bottle in the backseat of the priest's car.

"Have you been drinking, Father?"

"Only water," the priest replied.

The officer asked, "Then what is that bottle of wine in the backseat?"

The priest looked at the bottle, then looked up to heaven and said, "Good Lord, You've done it again!"

Now, even though Jesus did turn water into wine once, He wants to give you something even better better than wine. As it says in the Song of Solomon 1:2: "Let him kiss me with the kisses of his mouth; for your love is better than wine" (WEB).

Indeed, God's love *is* better than wine, and we can start expecting some great things to happen in our lives as we drink freely of His love.

Think of it this way: Why does a person enjoy wine? Well, not that I would know, but from what people have told me—wink, wink—when consumed in moderation, it makes you forget your past for a while, forget your mistakes, your inhibitions. You are much bolder, happier and more loving toward the people you are with.

And beyond the positive feelings it engenders, wine (again, when consumed in moderation) has some demonstrated health benefits.[5] It can lower your cholesterol, protect your heart with antioxidants, control blood sugar, boost your immune system and positively affect your brain, keeping your memory sharp. It can even help fend off a cold, fight cancer and help you lose weight. What a list!

This is *not* an argument for or against the drinking of alcohol. But I am trying to illustrate a point: that God's love confers far more benefits than wine does. His love gives you the strength to pray for the sick, the boldness to tell somebody that Jesus saved your life and the confidence to command demons to flee. God's love does not just temporarily dull pain—His love heals it permanently.

To sum up: Why is God's love better than wine?

◈ You can drink it without limit, without having to wonder if you have had too much.

◈ God's love does not cost anything. As we read in Isaiah 55:1: "All you who are thirsty, come and drink. . . . Come buy wine and milk without money and without cost" (NCV). I have counseled many people who lost fortunes because of their addictions to alcohol, drugs or gambling. But a happy, victorious life does not cost you. (It cost Jesus everything.) So you can drink and drink, and God never makes you pay the bill. His love and goodness are always "on the house." (Another round, anyone?!)

◈ God's love never turns you into a raging maniac or gives you a hangover. His love is refreshing and everlasting.

◈ Unlike alcohol and drugs, God's love has no side effects. So rather than getting wasted and feeling empty and regretful afterward, you feel renewed.

◈ His love makes you a better person because you are no longer trying to fill your voids or heal your hurts any other way. You have been healed and satisfied by the love of Jesus. So you no longer demand that people give you something you were designed to receive only from Him.

Healer of a Broken Heart

Now let's turn to the heart, the manufacturing center of our hopes, dreams and desires.

For the young, with innocent, loving hearts, it is easy to dream. Life seems filled with endless possibilities. They daydream about their future lives, imagining themselves as great astronauts, business owners, ballerinas, professional athletes—you name it.

But somewhere along the line, our hearts are broken, damaged or discouraged. And broken hearts lead to broken dreams. That is why we must protect our hearts. As King Solomon said in Proverbs 4:23, "Above all else, guard your heart, for everything you do flows from it" (NIV).

In order to protect the heart, we need to recognize three fundamental things that can break it: betrayal, rejection and disappointment.

Have you ever been betrayed?

Perhaps someone you trusted turned on you or lied about you. As the Scripture says in Psalm 41:9, "Even my close friend in whom I trusted, who ate my bread, has lifted his heel against me" (ESV). This certainly happened to Jesus near the end of his life.

But God will never betray you. He will never turn on you.

Have you ever been rejected?

The downward spiral of rejection goes something like this:

◈ You may be, at first, unable to speak.
◈ You then might feel dizzy or shaky.
◈ You have the powerful urge to run away.
◈ You are anxious about the future.

You feel this way because you are interpreting rejection through the lens of fear. And you are overinvested in someone else's opinion of you. A person's acceptance or rejection cannot act as a barometer of your self-love. In times of crisis, it is only when we love ourselves unconditionally (while understanding the pain of others) that the bitterness of rejection can fade away.

Remember: God knows every single thing about you, and He still loves you and accepts you. He will never reject you. As the Bible says, "My father and mother may abandon me, but the LORD will take care of me" (Psalm 27:10 GNT).

Have you ever been disappointed? Who hasn't, right?

Life often disappoints us. We run up against obstacles, competition and complications. People we had faith in disappoint us. And we sometimes disappoint ourselves. So instead of persisting, we eventually stop trying. Why? Because disappointment has crushed our hearts.

We lose our faith and ambition. Our dreams dissolve in despair. In this state of heartbreak, we shut down the dream center and settle for the nightmare within.

Here is the secret to pushing past disappointment. Psalm 43:5 says it all: "Why, my soul, are you downcast? . . . Put your hope in God" (NIV).

Indeed, the reason we are downcast and disappointed is that we put our hope in people rather than in God. We expect people to come through for us, help us, approve of us, treat us the way we want to be treated. In other words, our expectations of people are too high. And our expectations of God are too low. So that sets us up for disappointment.

> God knows every single thing about you, and He still loves you and accepts you.

But as we redirect our hope from people to God, we will stop living in disappointment. Romans 5:5 says, "Hope does not disappoint, because the love of God has been poured out within our hearts through the Holy Spirit." Notice God is *pouring* that love, not sprinkling it. This means you are going to be drenched in it. And that is when hope will soar again.

Indeed, the Holy Spirit's first intention in our lives is to reveal to us the love of God. Then, once we are secure in God's love, He comes upon us, and, as the Scripture says, "Your sons and your daughters shall prophesy, and your young men shall see visions and your Elders shall dream dreams" (Acts 2:17 ABPE). "The Spirit of the Lord is upon me," Jesus said, "because . . . he hath sent me to heal the brokenhearted, to preach deliverance to the captives, and recovering of sight to the blind, to set at liberty them that are bruised" (Luke 4:18 KJV).

Yes, our hearts are bruised, battered and even broken. But a new beginning is only a minute away. A mere shift in perspective—from feeling unloved and uncertain to being certain that God loves you—can bring healing. He is in love with you. You make Him happy just by being you and trusting Him.

So ask the Holy Spirit to reveal God's love and heal a heart broken by disappointment, betrayal and regret. Ask Him to show you "the extravagant dimensions of Christ's love" (Ephesians 3:18 MSG). Tell Him you want to "reach out and experience the breadth [of it]! Test its length! Plumb the depths! Rise to the heights! Live full lives, full in the fullness of God. . . . God can do anything, you know—far more than you could ever imagine or guess or request in your wildest dreams!" (verses 18, 20 MSG).

Are you ready for God to exceed your wildest dreams? Make a decision to declare this out loud for the next thirty days. You will be amazed at the results.

DECIDE AND DECLARE

◈ I will greet this day with God's love in my heart!

◈ When I feel discouraged, I will lift my hands to the Lord, and He will fill my mouth with song.

◈ Because of God's love, all those who seek to hurt me will be stopped, for love makes my shield of faith strong.

◈ God has a plan for my life and will provide for my every need.

◈ I will love all those I come in contact with today.

◈ I will love the weak and make them strong.

◈ I will love the inspired and be inspired by them.

◈ I will love the empty and help them be filled—I will love the filled, and they will overflow!

◈ I will love the broken, and they will be healed.

◈ Because God loves me, I will love myself.

NOW PRAY THIS WITH ME

Jesus, Your love is the secret to fulfillment, the source of all healing inside and out. It calms every storm. It silences every enemy. Your love fills every empty part of my soul, bringing me comfort.

When I face darkness, Your love brings light. When I'm overwhelmed, it inspires and encourages me. When I'm distressed, it reminds me of Your goodness. When it feels like heaven is silent, it reminds me that You know what I'm going through.

Your love will lead me. Your love will direct me. Your love will inspire me. Your love will heal me. Your love will fill me. Your love will revive me. Your love will deliver me from my enemies. It will protect me in times of danger. It will redirect the arrows of the wicked one.

Help me confront everyone I meet with love. Let Your love shine through my eyes, bring a smile to my lips and sound out through my voice. May Your love bring peace, lower people's defenses and empower them to experience Your presence. Because You love me, I will love myself. I will love others. And I will love life, no matter what I face. I will worship You this day with Your love in my heart.

Now, from this moment forward, I command fear and hate to leave my body and my mind. I command fear and hate, leave my family and my home, in Jesus' name!

5

The Gift That Costs Nothing

Do as the heavens have done, forget your evil;
With them forgive yourself.

William Shakespeare

He could hardly believe it. The most expensive car in the world had broken down in the middle of the road.

The owner, a wealthy man from England, was on vacation in France and had transported his brand-new Rolls-Royce across the English Channel with him. He felt confident that his most prized possession would provide total comfort and reliability on the trip. Except that it did not.

So there he was, enjoying an outing along the French Riviera, with a broken-down luxury car. And because of the car's complicated engine, no local mechanic could fix it.

Desperate, the man contacted Rolls-Royce headquarters. And would you believe that a Rolls-Royce mechanic flew over from England to handle the repairs?

The owner was expecting to receive a hefty bill for this service, but to his surprise, one never came. After several weeks, he sent a letter inquiring about it.

The Rolls-Royce representative's response arrived a few days later. It stunned him: "Thank you so much for your letter. You need to know that we have *no record* in our files of your car having broken down. In fact, neither your Rolls-Royce nor any Rolls-Royce has *ever* broken down—at *any* place, at *any* time, for *any* reason. Therefore, you owe us nothing and never will."

The lesson of this story is powerful: No matter what breaks down in our lives, our manufacturer—our master builder—fixes and forgives us by His grace.

Regardless of what we have done wrong, God wipes the slate clean. He maintains *no record* in his files against us; he holds no debt against us. This means we owe *nothing* for our sins, flaws and mistakes. And we never will. Through the precious blood of Jesus, God declares us forgiven.

> **Through the precious blood of Jesus, God declares us forgiven.**

He maintains *no record* in his files regarding our sins, mistakes, breakdowns and flaws. Think about that for a minute.

We no longer have to lie awake at night, beating ourselves up for what we did wrong or nursing a grudge against someone for what he or she did to us. Like the tide of the ocean, which erases our footprints in the sand, all is washed away and forgiven.

As the Scripture says in Romans 14:22: "Happy is the one who does not condemn himself." In other words, happy are those who know they are forgiven. Knowing this releases joy in your mind and in your heart.

Sadly, so often we do not see forgiveness for what it is—a gift. And neither do we accept this gift. The source of so much of our unhappiness can be traced to feeling unforgiven.

Now, before I go any further, I hope you can tell at this point that this chapter on forgiveness is not like any other you may have read. Because usually when someone talks about the word *forgiveness,* our

70

knee-jerk reaction is to feel bad about holding a grudge. Or maybe we are preparing ourselves to forgive someone.

But that is not what I am talking about. I am talking about *receiving* forgiveness. And while forgiving others is powerful, you do not need any strength to do so. Forgiving others is a reflex.

What do I mean by that? Well, forgiving others is an overflow of receiving God's forgiveness for ourselves. You cannot give what you do not have.

That is why I say again and again: The middle part of the word *forgiveness* is *give*. Forgiveness is a gift. And it originates with God. That is what empowers it to flow from us to other people—with a stop to forgive ourselves along the way.

All we have to do is accept it and say thank you.

It is God's *blessing*—paid in full through Jesus' blood. In fact, the root word for "blessing" is actually the Old English "blōd," or "blood." In other words, *every* "blessing" promised by God is found in the blood of Jesus. God is giving us everything—every favor, every blessing, every freedom—from our mistakes, from guilt, condemnation, inferiority and shame. And when we know this is truly an unconditional gift, it leads to true happiness and peace.

One of the most inspiring Bible passages I have ever read is "As far as east is from west—that is how far God has removed our sin from us" (Psalm 103:12 CEB).

> "As far as east is from west—that is how far God has removed our sin from us."

We all know that east and west, eternal opposites, are as far from each other as any two things can be. And that is how far away you are from your sins. All you have to do is receive the gift of forgiveness. **The *Amen* of any prayer means "so BE it" or "it is so." You see? Our only part is Amen. I'm pretty sure you can handle that part! Ha!**

Best of all, you can receive forgiveness before you think you deserve it, before you could possibly earn it, and even before you have apologized for whatever you've done. It is not something God is selling. He is giving it away. It is unconditional.

And when you accept it, the enemy loses his power over you. Whereas Satan keeps you in unforgiveness to get an advantage over you, God keeps you in forgiveness, turning a resentful soul into a healthy, loving one.

So what are you suffering from today? What secret have you told no one? What have you done that makes you feel condemned, too ashamed to accept forgiveness from God?

No matter what it is, forgiveness is yours to claim. It is a gift waiting for you, already sealed in Jesus' blood. And you do not have to go to confession to receive it. You simply need to go to God in your heart and say, "Father, I thank you for the gift of forgiveness. Thank you for forgiving my mistakes, my sins, my failures. I receive your mercy, grace and blessing today."

Yes, it is that simple. And by the way, in the acts of giving and receiving forgiveness, do not worry about your leftover feelings from the past. Were you right? Was the other person wrong? It does not matter anymore. Your feelings will not always be consistent with the facts.

The truth is, if you accept God's mercy, it is yours. The struggle is over. The feelings will catch up later. So do not wait for them. Get up, brush yourself off and move forward, as if your past were dead and gone. Why? Because it is.

As God promises in Hebrews 8:12, "Their sins and their iniquities I will remember no more" (KJV). *That* is His amazing grace. So why do we, as *imperfect* people, have such a hard time letting go of something a *perfect* God does not even remember? When you bring up your past with God, He has a two-word answer for you: *What past?*

Remember: Forgiving others flows from feeling forgiven, as illustrated in Colossians 3:13: "Forbearing one another, and forgiving one another, if any man have a quarrel against any: even as Christ forgave you, so also do ye" (KJV). This verse tells us two important things:

- *Jesus already forgave you.* Just accept that. Believe that.
- *Because He has forgiven you, you are empowered to forgive others.*

Do you see? It is not a command. It is a description of how forgiveness works. As you receive it freely, you are empowered to give it to yourself and others, which is one form of loving yourself.

"Mirror, Mirror, on the Wall"

Is there a connection between love and forgiveness? Simply put, one does not exist without the other.

Love for others can only exist if you have love for yourself. In fact, your reaction to God's gift of forgiveness is inseparable from your view of yourself.

So right now, if you go to the mirror and look yourself in the eye and do not like the person you see, there is only one thing to do: Forgive yourself.

So often what we see is someone who needs to be fixed, someone who is broken or defective, someone who is lacking, not as good as other people. But hear this: God made you to love yourself, and the enemy of your soul is self-hatred and condemnation.

That enemy is trying to convince you that you are not good enough, not attractive enough, not successful enough because of your imperfections. But what you are hearing is a lie. God wants to deliver you from this self-hatred and anger.

So when you look in that mirror, the problem is not that you are not holy enough or not good enough or not attractive enough or not successful enough. The problem is that you are not seeing yourself as God sees you—completely and radically forgiven. By the way, the word *radical* comes from the Latin *radix*, which means "root." You are forgiven from the root up.

Our failure to see ourselves as forgiven leads to guilt, condemnation, comparing and despairing rather than accepting God's gift. Remember that He created you and died for you so that He could have a relation-ship with you. And if the Prince of the universe, the King of kings, the Lord of lords wants to be with you, that means you are beautiful, valuable and amazing to Him.

So you need to let go and forgive yourself so you can start loving yourself the way God already loves you. And when you do, you are simply catching up to what God has already done. He has already forgiven you.

When you believe this, you will know that everything is going to be all right. Healing and happiness will flow like a river.

Eight Hundred Sons, One Father

In an old Spanish town near Madrid years ago, a father and son had a terrible falling-out.

The son bitterly turned away from his father and disappeared for a long, long time. But as soon as the son ran away, his father set out to find him. He searched and searched for months and months to no avail.

Finally, in a last desperate effort to locate him, the father placed an ad in a Madrid newspaper. It read: "My dear beloved Paco, meet me in front of this newspaper office at noon on Saturday. All is forgiven. I love you. Your father."

On Saturday, eight hundred Pacos showed up, looking for forgive-ness and love from their fathers.

Are there any other Pacos out there?

We are all Pacos. We have all run or hidden or thought we were too ashamed and guilty and broken to turn to God. Or turn back to God. But our heavenly Father says, *Meet with me today. All is forgiven. I love you. Your Father.* Wow!

We all crave forgiveness and instinctively know how powerful it is. It may not change the past, but it opens up an incredible future, one unhindered by your history of hurts and pains, grudges and regrets. No longer will you bring leftover anger into new relationships. No longer will you act out your hurt by being withdrawn, moody or even nasty.

Even better, when you receive and give forgiveness, you automatically cut off one of the main roads to addiction. You no longer need to numb the pain with smoking, drinking, drugs, prescription medicines, food, gambling—whatever. You are freed from the power of it all and can tap into the energy and faith that emerge when you are willing to give up the urge to strike back, to punish yourself and others.

This kind of all-encompassing forgiveness is life-changing. It is much more than just letting go of the past. It is moving beyond it—to the life you truly want, the one you thought was impossible, free from guilt and pain.

You might ask, *What about the people I need to forgive? What if they keep hurting me?* Well, sometimes we need to forgive people from afar, from a distance, right?

In other words, you forgive them, bless them and pray for them. But that does not mean you go back into business with them or that you continue a relationship with them, allowing them to mistreat you. No, that is just old-fashioned stupid. That is not forgiveness. That is self-abuse. You are not a punching bag for people in pain. You must choose your associations wisely and stay away from people who hurt you.

But you can nonetheless forgive. To do this takes a powerful dose of love. You must see the people who hurt you as God's creations—imperfect human beings with the same flaws and vulnerabilities we all have. But you forgive and then *let them go*. Rinse and repeat. Give that pardon. Let it go. People who hurt you do not hold power over you unless you allow them to. I promise you that when you forgive, you are well on your way to a satisfied life, the one of your dreams, the one that God intended for you all along.

"Take Two and Call Me in the Morning"

What are the benefits of forgiveness—of yourself and others?

For starters, forgiveness brings healing, physical and emotional.

In fact, studies have proved that the act of forgiveness lowers the risk of heart attack.[1] It lowers cholesterol and improves sleep; it reduces body pain and blood pressure; and it cuts down on anxiety, depression and stress. Huh? Talk about a magic pill with no side effects. That is why forgiveness is the most powerful pill in the universe.

What happens if we do not swallow the forgiveness pill?

We are trapped in the fight-or-flight response, the physiological reaction to perceived attacks. Our bloodstreams are instantly flooded with the high-stress hormones adrenaline and cortisol. Heart rate, blood pressure and immune response spike. These reactions increase the risk of all kinds of mental and physical ailments.

No wonder there are so many heart attacks in America—eight hundred thousand of them per year. In fact, heart disease accounts for one in four deaths, more than all types of cancers combined. Someone has a heart attack every forty seconds in America.[2]

What is causing this? Poor diet? Lack of exercise? Genetics? Those factors definitely increase the risk of coronary disease. But the greatest problem for a vulnerable heart is chronic stress. And, as Dr. Everett Worthington of Virginia Commonwealth University concluded, "Chronic unforgiveness causes stress. Every time people think of their transgressor, their body responds."[3]

That chemical storm of adrenaline and cortisol changes the way blood clots, which increases the risk of a heart attack. That is why your life may depend on forgiveness: A human heart can only take so much stress and pressure before it can no longer function.

Forgiveness also produces emotional healing. Dr. Karl Menninger once said that if he "could convince the patients in psychiatric hospitals that their sins were forgiven, 75 percent of them could walk out the next day."[4]

Dr. Bernie Siegel, a well-known scholar, surgeon and retired professor at Yale University, studied 57 terminally ill cancer patients and found a connection between forgiveness and remission. He wrote:

At a certain particular moment in time they decided that the anger and the depression were probably not the best way to go, since they had such a little bit of time left, and so they went from that to being loving, caring, no longer angry, no longer depressed, and able to talk to the people they loved. . . . And at that point the tumors started to shrink.[5]

When you add it all up, forgiveness is a magic pill that can work miracles, much better than any antidepressant. It transforms you physically and emotionally. Even the thought of it can lead to

◈ healthier relationships
◈ improved mental health
◈ less anxiety, stress and hostility
◈ fewer symptoms of depression
◈ a stronger immune system
◈ improved heart health
◈ improved self-esteem

Let's feel the forgiveness that God has given us and spread it around. And do it tonight, before you go to bed. As the apostle Paul said, "Be angry, and yet do not sin; do not let the sun go down on your anger" (Ephesians 4:26). Release all the concerns that pile up during the day, growing and festering in your soul. All that negative emotion eats away at us, damaging our hearts. Paul calls this syndrome a "root of bitterness" that "springs up and causes trouble, and by it many become defiled" (Hebrews 12:15 ESV).

A Soft Heart

When we forgive ourselves and others, when we let go of blame, it opens the pathway to a soft heart. And it is in this softness of heart that we begin to feel happiness. Forgiveness floods the soul with empathy, humility and affection for others.

Conversely, a hard or cold heart locks us out of feeling love for God—or for ourselves or anyone else. Instead, pain has frozen our hearts, preventing us from feeling empathy and hope.

Why is a soft heart so crucial? Because nowadays, coldheartedness has chilled our culture as never before. It makes people overly sensitive and unforgiving. We fume over little things or big; we complain and hold grudges.

In its most extreme state, coldheartedness makes people capable of snapping or losing it altogether. That loss of control opens up the floodgates: Bad decisions rush in, and good sense flows out. It is no coincidence that psychopaths, who have no regard for life and become heartless criminals, are called cold-blooded. Of course, we can imprison criminals, and should, but it will not soften their hearts.

This reminds me of Matthew 24:12: "Because lawlessness is increased, most people's love will become cold." Consider the word *cold*—the definition of the Greek word *psykhros*, which perhaps also forms the root of the word *psyche*.[6] (Now we know where the word *psychopath* comes from.) And it all starts with a cold or hard heart.

If you feel like you might have some of the symptoms of a cold heart, I want you to realize that the remedy for a cold heart is love. And God's love will melt the coldest, hardest heart. Allow it to wash over you again and again. Flood your mind with God's love and his gift of forgiveness. It will begin to soften your heart and make you ready to forgive anyone who has hurt you, just as God has forgiven us. Even better, read the words below and on the next page aloud—they will help reinforce your connection to God's gift.

Ready for your breakthrough? Remember that forgiveness starts with a decision and is enforced with words. As it says in Proverbs 18:21, "Death and life are in the power of the tongue" (KJV). As you read aloud the declaration of forgiveness below, expect to experience the freedom Jesus paid for you to possess.

DECIDE AND DECLARE

◈ I forgive myself for failing and falling short.
◈ I forgive myself for letting the wrong people into my life.

◈ I forgive myself for not being a better person.

◈ I forgive myself for the selfish choices I have made that have hurt myself and others.

◈ I forgive myself for not being the best version of myself and robbing people of the beauty of what would have been.

◈ I forgive the people who let me down.

◈ I forgive the family members who hurt me with their anger, addictions and selfishness.

◈ I forgive those who said they would be my friends but then disappeared.

◈ I forgive people who have taken advantage of me, thought poorly of me and treated me as less valuable than God intended.

Now Pray This with Me

Holy Sprit, I receive Your healing from the self-sabotage and self-hatred I've allowed into my soul. Release me from feelings of being damaged, inadequate and unworthy. I ask You to restore the time and opportunities I may have lost.

Help me let go of regret and of guilt over the times I let other people down. Help me let go of painful memories so I can remember better times. And help me let go of anger so I can make room for new friendships.

Lift me up, so I am no longer a victim but instead I am more than a victor through You. Thank You for the gift of forgiveness, which I give to myself and others freely, just as You gave it to me!

6

The Two Most Powerful
Words on Earth

I would maintain that thanks are the highest form of
thought; and that gratitude is happiness doubled by
wonder.

G. K. Chesterton

He had seen himself the same way all his life. For as long as he could remember, it plagued him. The despair, the pain, the rejection, the hopelessness never left him, day or night.

So one day he and nine of his friends, who all suffered from leprosy, decided to make one last desperate attempt at a new and better life. They went to the man they knew as a healer. "Jesus, Master, have mercy on us," they cried.

"Go show yourself to the priests," Jesus told them.

And as they went, all of them were healed. It was truly a miracle. Yet only one of these ten men turned back to say thank you.

Why? How could that be? All ten of them were healed, but only one turned back.

Let me show you what made the difference.

"One of them, *when he saw* that he was healed, came back to Jesus, shouting, 'Praise God!' He fell to the ground at Jesus' feet, thanking him for what he had done. This man was a Samaritan" (Luke 17:15–16 NLT, emphasis added).

Notice "when he *saw* that he was healed."

All of them were healed, but this one saw it. This one was focused on what had just happened. The others went on with trying to obey the command to show themselves to the priests.

But this one, he stopped to *focus* on what had been done. His attention was completely arrested by the miracle that had just happened.

How many of us have experienced a miracle in life but are still focused on what we do *not* have? How many of us have taken the time to stop, look and focus on what God *has* given us?

This is the route to true happiness and fulfillment. This is the secret to an emotionally healthy life—focusing on the things you have right now. This is what leads to joy.

I am not just talking about adopting a thankful attitude or having good manners by saying thank you. That is all well and good, but it can hide ingratitude in the soul. I'm talking about what's underneath the surface—the invisible energy that flows through our minds and hearts, the underestimated force that powers a mighty waterfall of miracles—what we focus on. I cannot emphasize this enough. We get so focused on what we do not have that we rob ourselves of the gratitude that brings so much more into our lives. Funny how that works. When we are focused on what we do not have, it often eludes our grasp. But when we focus on what God has already given us, somehow this attracts the things we need without our even asking for them.

When the Samaritan was healed of leprosy, only one thing mattered to him: thanking the one who made him well. He took the time to notice, to see, to focus on what God had just done.

Jesus went on to say, "Didn't I heal ten men? Where are the other nine? Has no one returned to give glory to God except this foreigner?" (verses 17–18 NLT). (The Samaritan did not grow up in the same

81

religious tradition as the other nine did. He was a nonbeliever, but Jesus' miracle sure changed all that.)

"And Jesus said to the man, 'Stand up and go. Your faith has healed you'" (verse 19 NLT).

> Thankfulness is the highest form of faith.

Notice that Jesus said "your faith." All the man did differently was *see* that he was healed and turn back to give thanks. Jesus equated thanks with faith.

In other words, thankfulness is the highest form of faith. When you are thankful, you are a magnet for whatever you need in life.

Fear versus Faith

I always say that thankfulness is the result of "thinkfulness." What you focus on you will eventually feel.

I guarantee that if you focus on your deficiencies or on the faults of others or on what you lack, you will work yourself into a state of despair, bitterness, anxiety and fear. But the thoughts you fill your mind with will determine the positive or negative energy that will carry you into or out of the next great season of your life.

Fear focuses on all the things that have gone wrong or could go wrong; gratitude focuses on all the things that have gone right—or will go right.

So we get to choose what we give our attention to and how we will look at any given situation. Gratitude, like forgiveness, becomes an emotional reflex. The more you look for the good, the more thankful you become. You are transformed by it and feel happier because of it.

That is why "counting your blessings" is no old wives' tale (no offense to wives 😄). It is vital; it is emotional nourishment. It activates your faith, frees your mind and awakens your genius. It heals the body, improves relationships and promotes leadership qualities, too.

David said in Psalm 103:2, "Bless the LORD, O my soul, and forget none of His benefits" (NASB1995).

Thankful choices—such as appreciating the positive people God has put into your life—are always the best choices. Your friends and supporters help make you the best version of yourself. Thanking them with a word, a text, a thank-you note is a simple but powerful gesture.

As a matter of fact, that is what the book of Philippians is—a thank-you letter from Paul to the people of Philippi, who helped him spread the Gospel with their prayers and gifts. And get this: He wrote it *while he was in prison.*

Paul starts his letter with "I give thanks to my God for every remembrance of you, always praying with joy for all of you in my every prayer" (Philippians 1:3–4 CSB).

Think about that. Even though he was imprisoned for preaching the Gospel, he did not let his circumstances dictate what he believed or poison his attitude toward the people in his life—or poison his life at all. What was his antidote to the bitterness in that prison cell? Gratitude.

So often, we lose perspective because our focus is on our predicament rather than on our power. Paul also wrote these legendary words: "For God has not given us a spirit of fear, but of power and of love and of a sound mind" (2 Timothy 1:7 NKJV).

Notice the antidote to fear that Paul prescribed: *What you have been given neutralizes what you have not been given.* Power, love and a sound mind neutralize fear. And God has already given you these things. Your recognition, appreciation and declaration of them is what vanquishes fear.

Scrambled Eggs

It reminds me of the man who sat down for breakfast as his wife prepared him a beautiful three-course meal. He took one look at it and said, "You scrambled the eggs! I wanted them over easy!" (Maybe you remember the movie *Anger Management*, in which there is a similar scene between Jack Nicholson and Adam Sandler: "I said *over easy!*" Nicholson screams as he throws a plate of eggs against the wall.)

So the next day the wife made exactly what her husband wanted: eggs over easy. He took one look at them and said, "I thought I told you I like my eggs scrambled!" She thought, *I can't win with this guy. I know what I'll do.*

The day after that she made one egg scrambled and one egg over easy. *There! That'll fix him*, she thought.

The husband saw his new breakfast and barked, "What's the matter with you, woman? You scrambled the wrong one!"

This guy's "eggs" were truly scrambled. Yet how many of us are always finding something to be negative about? We are looking for the bad rather than looking for the good.

You see, we do not have the power to live a trouble-free life. But we *do* have the power to live a negativity-free life. How? By deciding what we will look for in any given situation. This will free you from the mentality of life happening *to* you, and you will start discovering that life is happening *for* you.

The pandemic of 2020 ushered in an unprecedented period of loss, death, economic stress and uncertainty. But amid all the chaos, I heard the voice of God say, *Look for the good.* Even in the middle of that crisis, we were given an opportunity to reprioritize our lives. To take care of what really matters—other people. And to lean in to trusting God in ways we never did before.

So while thankfulness is a weapon against the enemy of negativity, thanklessness is an emotional knife trying to slash and cut out all our happiness. But all that is about to change for you.

Unthankfulness is a sign of the times. Paul wrote in 2 Timothy 3:1–5 (NIV):

> There will be terrible times in the last days. People will be lovers of themselves, lovers of money, boastful, proud, abusive, disobedient . . . ungrateful, unholy, without love, unforgiving, slanderous, without self-control, brutal, not lovers of the good, treacherous, rash, conceited,

lovers of pleasure rather than lovers of God—having a form of godliness but denying its power. Have nothing to do with such people.

Little has changed in two thousand years. Those are some serious toxic behaviors in that list. But notice that one little word in the middle of it all: *ungrateful*.

At the center of so much of our pain, so many of our negative emotions, is unthankfulness. And the verse tells us to have nothing to do with unthankful people. But first, let's have nothing to do with *being* unthankful people.

Notice that the passage says that unthankful people have "a form of godliness" but deny its power. This means that when we choose to focus on what we do not have, we deny the power of gratitude. When we use gratitude as an instrument of healing our souls, however, we release its power to make us happy and healthy.

Imagine that your favorite team is playing in the Super Bowl or World Cup—and you are invited. You are treated to the best seats along with unlimited refreshments. But you are given all this under one condition: You are not allowed to applaud your team or stand and cheer or celebrate its scores or its victory. You have to just sit there.

You see? You would not enjoy what you could not praise. The true fulfillment of anything is in the praising of that thing. A great meal causes you to praise it. A great concert causes you to applaud it. But if you take praise out of the equation, there is no fulfillment. There is no true happiness. The delight is incomplete until it is expressed.

As simple as that is to understand, so often we forget to praise and thank God even for the little things. We rob ourselves of meaning in life—the praise of a thing. Happiness comes from focusing on the things that make us praise and celebrate God and His people. And that is our true purpose of life—to praise, glorify and thank God.

As the Scripture says in Romans 1:21, "Although they knew God, they did not glorify Him as God, nor were thankful, but became futile in their thoughts, and their foolish hearts were darkened" (NKJV).

So yes, ungratefulness leads to a life of futility, potentially foolish decisions and mental disorders—subjects I will address in part II of this book.

To glorify God means to magnify Him. A magnifying glass does not make the object it is focused on bigger. It just makes it *appear* bigger from a close perspective. We cannot make God bigger than He already is, but we can focus on what He has done for us, and He will become bigger in our eyes.

In that sense, giving thanks and praise is one of the greatest spiritual weapons God has given us in the battles of life. True, the enemy of our souls wants to defeat us, to keep us worried, angry, upset and afraid, but praising what we are grateful for disarms that enemy, celebrates the victory and brings us into the will of God, to the purpose for which we were born.

> Giving thanks and praise is one of the greatest spiritual weapons God has given us in the battles of life.

As it says in Revelation 4:11: "Thou art worthy, O Lord, to receive glory and honour and power: for thou hast created all things, and for thy pleasure they are and were created" (KJV).

In other words, you were created to be pleasing to God. How? By thanking Him for the gifts He has given.

So first and foremost, praise God for what He has done for you—and what He is *going* to do for you. Expectation is a powerful force. By remembering what *has* been done, you will activate your faith in what *can* be done.

So start sending up praise for the miracle you're going to receive, for the best friend you're going to meet, for the child you are going to have, for the career God is going to open the door for. When you do, you will experience an instant feeling of well-being and confident trust.

You see, the heart of thanks and praise grows from the core of humility, derived from the Latin word *humus*, which means "earth." A down-to-earth person lets go of entitlement, conceit and pride. A down-to-earth person looks for the good in everything and every person. And a down-to-earth person sees the good in life as a gift from God. Humility allows you to truly be thankful and become the best version of yourself.

In humility, we can give thanks for even the littlest things—the air we breathe, the clothes on our backs and the food on our tables. So when you have a great meal, give praise. When you watch your child playing, give praise. When you receive a gift from someone, give praise. In fact, praise and glorify God in everything.

When you are on top of the mountain, give Him glory, because He *got* you there.

When you are in the bottom of the valley, give Him glory because He is *with* you there.

You will find that praise is a reflex action of the grateful heart, a sign that God has been good to you. So in this way we discover that praise does not merely express our enjoyment. It also completes it. To put it another way, when you are focused on the good God has done for you, your natural response is gratitude and praise.

The Gateway to the Miraculous

What if I told you that thankfulness is an engine that drives miracles?

This power of thanks is vastly underrated and underused. The result? A mundane and average existence. But God can "do above and beyond all that we ask or think according to the power that works in us" (Ephesians 3:20 CSB).

What is that power that works within us, creating the "above and beyond all that we can ask or think"? It is the power of *thank you*.

Let me give you two simple examples.

When Jesus fed five thousand people with five loaves of bread and two fish, it was obviously miraculous. Notice how it happened.

Jesus said, *Let's feed this multitude of people.*

The disciples asked how.

Jesus asked, *What do you already have?*

They said there was a little boy there with five loaves and two fish. But what was that gonna accomplish?

"Then Jesus took the loaves, gave thanks to God, and distributed them to the people. Afterward he did the same with the fish. And they all ate as much as they wanted" (John 6:11 NLT).

Notice that Jesus only had five loaves. What did He do with them? He gave thanks to God. The only other things Jesus had were two fish. What did He do with them? He gave thanks to God.

What happened then? "They all ate as much as they wanted." Wow! Thanks for what He *had* produced the miracle of what He *needed*.

Thank God for whatever you have. It will become as much as you want or need. In short, awaken to the so-called little things in life that are not so little after all. Magnifying what you have multiplies what you have. Thanks multiplies the good in life.

Are you going through a crisis and need a breakthrough? A miracle of some kind? I have great news for you, which leads to my second example of the power of thank you. It starts with a story you are probably familiar with—the story of Lazarus. But there is something in it you might not have noticed before.

Lazarus was the brother of Mary and Martha. When he got sick, Mary and Martha were emotionally crushed because they loved their brother so much. But the first secret to the miracle they needed was what happened in John 11:3: "The sisters sent word to him, saying, 'Lord, behold, the one whom you love is sick'" (LEB).

Notice that Mary and Martha did not focus on how much Lazarus loved Jesus. They focused on how much Jesus loved *him*. In the same way, your breakthrough and miracle start with your absolute confidence that Jesus loves *you*, which directly leads to being thankful and happy.

So often, we feel like we have to love God more in order to be worthy of His miracle. But that's not how God operates. He wants you to know how much He loves you, and that is the "why" behind God's power. He will do it because He loves you.

When Jesus received word about Lazarus's illness from Mary and Martha, He did not go to Lazarus right away. He waited days, and during the delay, Lazarus died. This seems a a little strange when you think about it, that Jesus would let Lazarus's condition worsen. Haven't we all felt like that at times? That if God really loves us, why does our situation grow worse at times? But something I have learned in my own life is that God's timing is always perfect, and it is never too late for God, no matter how bad the situation is. When we take care of the trusting, God takes care of the timing.

Even though Lazarus died, his story did not end in death. And no matter how bad your situation is, no matter how dead everything seems or looks, it is not over with God.

When Jesus arrived at Lazarus's tomb, He was moved with compassion for His good friend. "Take away the stone," He said.

"But, Lord," said Martha, the sister of the dead man, "he has been there four days."

Then Jesus said, "Did I not tell you that if you believe, you will see the glory of God?" (John 11:39–40 NIV).

Jesus was giving Martha the second secret to the miracle breakthrough she needed. If you believe, you will see! Faith works through love. In other words, miracles happen in an atmosphere of faith. When you believe, you will see.

So first, know that you are loved.

Second, believe *before* you see.

And the third secret to your miracle breakthrough shows up in verse 41, after the stone in front of Lazarus's tomb had been taken away. Jesus looked up and said, "Father, I thank you that you have heard me. I knew that you always hear me, but I said this for the benefit of the people standing here, that they may believe that you sent me" (verses 41–42 NIV).

Notice what Jesus did not say: "Father, help Me" or, "Father, give Me the power" or, "Father, will You?"

He said, "Father, I thank You."

The secret to His faith was His gratitude. When Jesus said those powerful words, He was expressing the highest form of faith.

"Now when He had said these things, He cried with a loud voice, 'Lazarus, come forth!' And he who had died came out bound hand

and foot with graveclothes, and his face was wrapped with a cloth" (verses 43–44 NKJV).

Jesus already knew that God would raise Lazarus from the dead. He knew that God would answer His prayer because Jesus knew that God is always listening, and that is why Jesus was thankful. He knew that thankfulness is the gateway to miracles.

God wants to work miracles in your life. He does it by faith. And faith is most fully expressed in our gratitude for what He has promised *before* we ever see it. It was paid for at the cross. And that is what makes it so simple to receive.

And through the power of these two transcendent words, *thank you*, we have an opportunity to live a miraculously blessed life.

A Checkup from the Neck Up

It is so simple: Thankfulness is a spiritual antidote to anger, negativity, pessimism, sadness, jealousy, resentment and bitterness. Scientific studies have proved that giving thanks affects us in many powerful ways.

- ◈ You sleep better at night and wake up refreshed.
- ◈ You get sick less often.
- ◈ You exercise more.
- ◈ You activate your built-in stress-buffering ability.
- ◈ You feel more enthusiasm for daily tasks.
- ◈ You are more productive and creative at work.
- ◈ You are more confident and relaxed.
- ◈ You are less depressed.
- ◈ You have more energy.
- ◈ You are more empathetic.
- ◈ You are less envious.
- ◈ You are a better problem solver.

- ◈ You are more likable.
- ◈ You make better decisions.
- ◈ You deal with adversity more effectively.
- ◈ You build stronger relationships.
- ◈ You are more motivated and optimistic.
- ◈ You are less materialistic.
- ◈ You have lower levels of inflammation, thereby strengthening the heart.
- ◈ You lower your blood pressure.
- ◈ You raise your tolerance for pain.
- ◈ You prevent stress related conditions such as ulcers, back pain, headaches and cramps.

When you look at that list, all you can say is, *Wow!*

The cure to so much of what ails us is to be grateful, to be thankful for what God has done in our lives. In a state of gratitude, it is nearly impossible to become violent or to stay angry, offended or depressed. Instead, you are motivated to see the best in life, not the worst.

Remember: What God has done for you is greater than what people have done to you.

It is all about what you focus on.

The victim mentality is a waste of soul power. And many of us have spent too long nursing and rehearsing our pain. Yes, you might have been mistreated or wronged, but God can more than make up for it. I promise that remembering the good God has done for you will produce joy.

> Remembering the good God has done for you will produce joy.

Did you know that certain human emotions, such as gratitude, activate the "pleasure center" of our brains?

This is the the so-called reward circuit, which lets us know when something is highly enjoyable. It can be turned on by anything from prayer to Scripture meditation, from chocolate to wine, from falling in love to exercising, from volunteer work to laughter.

When we anticipate or experience intense pleasure, the brain miraculously releases four types of neurotransmitters or "feel-good" chemicals[1]—dopamine, serotonin, oxytocin and endorphins. Think of these as the chemical quartet responsible for happiness. These natural boosters alleviate feelings of anxiety, depression and loneliness. They also help you avoid procrastination.

◈ Dopamine controls the brain's pleasure and reward systems, releasing positive feelings when you are expecting a reward.[2]

◈ Serotonin is the "happy chemical" that helps regulate mood and social behavior, appetite and digestion, sleep, and sexual desire and function. It is a mood stabilizer.

◈ Oxytocin is associated with a loving touch and close relationships, allowing us to feel close and bonded to others. (Yes, you can hug your way to happiness!)

◈ Endorphins are produced by the body to relieve stress and pain, a natural opioid. What boosts levels of endorphins? Vigorous exercise (the "runner's high"), generosity, even dark chocolate and laughter, among other things.

In other words, if you are in a good mood, you have got serotonin and dopamine to thank. If you have to "power through" a crisis, your endorphins are the heroes. And if you are feeling deeply in love, oxytocin is the culprit.

All in all, when these chemicals are released, they trigger a sense of euphoria. And amazingly, they can be activated on command. Even asking the question *What do I have to be grateful for?* is enough to change your brain chemistry.

In scientific terms, gratitude stimulates the hypothalamus (a part of the brain that regulates stress) and the ventral tegmental area (part of our "reward circuitry," which produces the sensation of pleasure).

So when you express gratitude, just this simple act increases serotonin production in the brain. And you immediately feel happier. In that sense, gratitude is the most powerful medication on earth, both a natural antidepressant and an anti-anxiety "drug." Turns out you have got the cure to depression and anxiety right in the medicine chest of your soul.

And it has been proved in study after study that a mind full of thankfulness, an attitude of gratitude, improves moods and reduces the stress hormone cortisol. Other studies note that regularly expressing gratitude not only changes the brain's chemistry, but it also literally changes its molecular structure.[3]

In short, like Prozac, gratitude heals us. And the best thing is that it does not come in a bottle. It is free. What is more, when you swallow the gratitude pill, there are no side effects except contentment and joy.

So as the Scripture says in Romans 12:2, "Be transformed by the renewing of your mind" (NIV), which to me refers to the rewiring of your brain that is accomplished in large part to flooding our soul with this powerful medicine called thankfulness.

The Missing Connection

We get off track at times, seeking pleasure in the wrong places in order to stimulate feel-good chemicals, right?

But pleasure itself was God's idea—the words *Garden of Eden* have become synonymous with "garden of pleasure." So addictions and compulsions are simply driven by our search for that pleasure (and, just as often, relief from pain). We have all used food, gambling, drugs, alcohol or sex to give us the temporary high that triggers the release of dopamine and other feel-good chemicals.

As I shared earlier, I was one of those people seeking pleasure and escape from pain before I fell in love with Jesus. Once that dopamine and serotonin hit the pleasure center of my brain, I was happy for a while. And that is why I returned to those things again and again.

I did not have the self-awareness to understand what was really driving me. I was unaware of my connection to God. Nor was I feeling grateful for what I *did* have. Instead, I found myself in a sea of despair. Trust me: Gratitude and thankfulness would have worked a lot better.

But then my entire life turned around once I accepted God's grace and began to appreciate His love and the gifts He gave me. This became the antidote for my depression and anxiety.

Would antidepressants have worked just as well? I do not believe so. I am not saying there is anything wrong with medication. And if a situation calls for medical help, by all means seek it. But medication cannot get to the root of things and produce lasting peace. Gratitude can.

The Gateway to Gratitude

The next time you find yourself going down the road of complaint and ingratitude, just stop. Freeze in the moment, then pivot from negative to positive, even if only temporarily. Ask yourself, *What do I have to be grateful for?* (And once you start making a list, you'll be surprised by how long it really is.)

As a follow up to that question, here are seven ways to unleash the power of gratitude.

1. Keep a gratitude journal.

Oprah Winfrey said that keeping a gratitude journal was the single best decision she ever made in her life. (And the multibillionare media empress has made a lot of great ones.) A gratitude journal is a powerful way to stay focused on the gifts God has given you. When you keep a journal, the dopamine cycle kicks right in. Your brain says, *Hey, I feel great after focusing on this. Go get me more of it!*

2. Write a thank-you note.

In this electronic age, a handwritten thank-you note is a gift to anyone who receives it. It is humanizing and gracious and can nurture your relationship with the recipient by expressing your appreciation of that person's impact on your life. Even if it is not handwritten, make a habit of sending at least one gratitude note or email a day to friends, family or colleagues, thanking them for what they do. (And once in a while, send one to yourself.)

3. Number your blessings.

We have all heard the expression "Count your blessings." Well, I am proposing that you do that literally. Take a few minutes once a week to make a list of what you are grateful for—what went right during the past seven days. Give each item on the list a number. Sometimes it helps to pick a number in advance—such as three or five or seven—and make sure you write down one thing next to each number.

4. Pray.

Pray about anything making you feel anxious or depressed. The Bible gives us the medicine for anxiety. Treat it as a signal to pray! Prayer with thanksgiving activates the peace of God in your heart and in your mind.

As you do, your metabolism slows, your heart rate and blood pressure decrease and your breath becomes calmer. Adding the power of thanksgiving to the power of prayer will bring freedom from sadness and relief from anxiety. Take a moment to thank God for the answer you need. Thank Him for turning your bad fortune into good. Thank Him for leading you by His Spirit into His perfect will.

5. Give your children a lesson in gratitude.

If you are a parent, it is never too late and never too early to teach your children a life lesson. Ask them at bedtime to tell you one or two things they did during the day that they feel thankful for, then get them to name a couple of people who mean something to them and whom they can thank God for.

6. Leave a trail of happiness wherever you go.

Remember, gratitude is the acknowledgment of things received, a focus on what you already have. So no matter where your day takes you, practice gratitude. From the subway to the restaurant, from school to home, from your office to the grocery store, be grateful and kind to everyone you meet. Thank the server who brought your food to the table, and thank your spouse for sticking with you another day. Rather than taking the people around you for granted, thank them for the little things they do.

7. Find a gratitude partner.

You do not have to practice thankfulness alone. It is helpful to partner up with a friend, family member or someone in your church. Every day, go over what you are both thankful for. It may sound corny, but the buddy system supports both people and keeps gratitude going.

Remember, "He who did not spare His own Son, but delivered Him over for us all, how will He not also with Him freely give us all things?" (Romans 8:32). And remember that when you say, "Father, I thank You," there is literally a signal sent through the neurotransmitters of your brain that hits the pleasure center. *Boom!* If you do not believe it, try it.

Now you know a little more about how the two most powerful words on earth can transform your life in every way.

DECIDE AND DECLARE

- ◈ Today, I shift my focus from what I do not have to what I *do* have.
- ◈ When I focus on God's blessings, I create gratitude in my life.
- ◈ I am not a victim but a victor.

◈ Life is happening *for* me—not *to* me.

◈ I will continue to look for the good in my life.

Now Pray This with Me

God, You have blessed me with Your life, Your love and Your goodness. You have not given me the spirit of fear, but You have given me power, love and a sound mind. Therefore I lack nothing.

Help me shift my perspective on life by looking for the good, remembering the good and expecting the good. I thank You, heavenly Father, that You love me, You've heard me and You're working all things out for my good! Amen.

7

You Are Worth It All

Long lay the world in sin and error pining.
'Til He appeared and the soul felt its worth.

"O Holy Night"

I n 2017, something extraordinary happened at Christie's, the legendary auction house, which sells some of the greatest treasures of the art world.

In a historic moment, the gavel came down on a record-breaking sale. Sold to the highest bidder was Leonardo da Vinci's *Salvator Mundi* (Savior of the world), which went for $450 million—the most expensive painting in the world.

But beyond the sale of a work so precious, many paintings housed in museums never come up for auction at all. Why not? Because they are considered priceless. For example, da Vinci's *Mona Lisa* is insured for $830 million, though its true value is incalculable. It will never be sold to anyone.

So let's take a look at you. What are you worth? What is your value?

Or to put it another way, if I were to ask, "What is your most precious possession?" I wonder what your answer would be. Would it be your family? Your physical health? Your life savings? Your dog?

To answer that question, look no further than Mark 8:36: "What does it profit a man to gain the whole world and forfeit his soul?" (ESV). In other words, Jesus is saying that the *human soul* has more value than all the riches of the world! So even when you don't value your soul in that way yet, God does! And we need to get a more accurate estimation of our soul's worth.

I am here to tell you that when you feel discouraged, depressed, unappreciated or even downright worthless, God's gavel has come down on a different verdict. In His loving eyes, you are the *Mona Lisa* of the world (much better looking though 😊). To Him, your value is beyond calculation.

No amount of money could even come close to the value of God's creation—*you*.

Yet how often do we feel undervalued, underestimated or insignificant? Maybe you derive your sense of worth from the opinion of others—your family, your friends, your coworkers. And when their judgment of you falls, so does yours.

Some days when you look in the mirror, you might feel defective, defeated, deserted or deprived. Maybe you think you lack the intelligence, achievement, popularity, good looks or good health that others have. These misconceptions feed low self-esteem, which can be debilitating, if not crippling.

So how can you increase your sense of self-worth from the inside out? I can tell you that it is not by anything you do. As I said before, you are not a human doing but a human being. Constant productivity will not increase your value, for happiness is not equivalent to achievements or monetary gain. Instead, your sense of self-worth is entirely dependent on the revelation of the worth of your soul. Truly grasping this changes everything. As we elevate our estimation of our soul's worth, we elevate everything else in our lives. Because as it says in the Scripture, "I pray that in every way you may prosper . . . [in direct proportion to how] your soul also prospers" (3 John 2 BSB).

> You are not a human doing but a human being.

The soul is not physical. It does not matter how old you are or what you look like or how much money you make. Your age, your health and your looks have nothing to do with it. The mirror might as well not exist, because God does not measure by appearances.

Your flesh and body, your skin and bones, are only a covering, a shell, a tent that you dwell in (see 2 Corinthians 5:1–8). Your body cannot do any of the things your soul can.

In simple words, your soul is the *real you*. It is your unique personality, the traits and characteristics that make you invaluable. And that soul is far more important and more powerful than anything in this world.

God Spoke to Me about You

Whether you are a Christian or someone who has never had a spiritual experience, you will be able to relate to what I am about to say.

Have you ever been swept up by the music at a great concert or worship service? I know you will agree that there is nothing quite like the energy and passion that music can create.

At a recent church service, I had just such a moment, one that affected me deeply, when the band started to play a worship song that declared *God was worthy of it all.* Those words stuck out to me. God is worthy of all our praise. He has given us the greatest gift in Jesus, and He has made the ultimate demonstration of love—dying for us, sacrificing Himself so that we could truly live.

> He has made the ultimate demonstration of love—dying for us, sacrificing Himself so that we could truly live.

He really is worthy of it all. The Creator of the universe, the Creator of our souls, is worthy to be thanked, praised, honored and glorified in whatever way resonates with you.

As we were all singing, I heard a voice speak clearly to my heart. In that moment, I knew it was the voice of God saying, *Yes, Son, I am worthy of it all. But let me tell you something: YOU are worth it all.*

Those words captivated me.

God said to me, "*Tell My people that they are worth it all. They are the reason I did everything I did.*"

When Jesus died for us, He was not dying for trash or worthless lowly creatures. He valued us. He saw the true worth inside of each of us, and that is why He gave His all for us.

God went on to say to me, *Awaken My people's sense of worth. Help them see that I did everything I did because of the value I place on each of them. They are worth it all!*

This changed my life, and I hope it changes yours.

The Creator, God Himself, is the smartest being in the universe. He is undoubtedly perfect in every way. And even though we have all sinned and fallen short of His perfection, He values us so much that He bought us back from sin and our failings with the only price He deemed fitting—His very own perfect blood. No other price would do.

The value of a thing is determined by how much the astute buyer is willing to pay. God paid for us with his own blood. That is value. And that is why you are worth it all to Him.

You Are Twice His

Each day, I try to remind myself of those words—that He is worthy of all my praise and that I am worth the sacrifice He made. And so are you—regardless of any feelings you have of unworthiness or self-judgment.

But so often, the lyrics we are hearing in our heads are negative and self-defeating. The song is out of tune. We have penned our own compositions, our own deluded ways of measuring our worth.

And in a culture consumed with comparisons, self-criticism becomes the enemy of the soul, a demonic voice that tells you, *You're not enough. You're lacking. You're worthless.*

Allow me to share a story that illustrates the essence of this chapter. As you read along, I hope your heart swells with gratitude and love, just as mine does when I recall it.

Many years ago, nine-year-old Bobby sat alone for hours and hours, carving a little sailboat out of wood. When he was finally finished working, he hurriedly carried the new boat to the edge of the river near his house.

He carefully placed the boat in the water and marveled at how smoothly it sailed. For the next hour, he sat in the warm sunshine, admiring that little boat, which he had built all by himself. But suddenly a strong gust of wind whipped up along the water. The boat became caught in a current. Bobby tried to pull it back to shore on the string it was attached to, but the string broke. And the little boat raced downstream.

He ran along the shore as fast as he could. But his little boat soon slipped out of sight. Bobby had lost his most prized possession. All afternoon he searched for it, to no avail. Finally, when it was too dark to look any longer, Bobby gave up and sadly walked home.

A few days later, on the way back from school, he spotted a boat that looked just like his in a store window. When he got closer, he could see . . . sure enough, it was his.

Bobby hurried to the store manager. "Sir," he said, "that's my boat in your window! I made it!"

"Sorry, son," the manager replied. "Someone else brought that boat in this morning. They said they found it down by the river. If you want it, you will have to buy it for five dollars."

Bobby did not give it a second thought. He ran home as fast as he could and counted all the money he had. Exactly five dollars. He ran back to the store, rushed to the counter and said, "Here's the money for my boat. It's mine!"

As he left the store, Bobby hugged his little boat tightly and said, "Now you're *twice* mine. First I made you, then I bought you!"

Think about those words: "First I made you, then I bought you."

If you ever feel like you are not worth much or that your mistakes have destroyed your value, or if you just feel insignificant, I want you to realize how God feels about you.

Like Bobby's little boat, you are twice His.

First He Made You, Then He Bought You

He paid the highest price, His blood, to buy you back from your pain, your past, your mistakes, your sins, your heartaches. And just like Bobby, God was happy and eager to do it. He bought you back from the dominion of the devil and the destruction the enemy attempted to weave into your precious soul.

So often, people have been beaten down by their mistakes, making them feel like they do not have value. The way we feel about ourselves is dictated by a confused culture that paralyzes the soul—that worships everything on the outside and treasures very little on the inside. We mistakenly believe that our self-worth is determined by our net worth, our physical beauty or lack thereof, by our IQ, our college degrees, our bank accounts, the size of our homes and cars, the number of likes on our social media accounts—or some other status symbol.

All wrong. I am here to tell you that your value is not determined by any of those exterior things. Instead, just as market conditions determined the worth of that Da Vinci painting sold at auction, your truth worth is determined by the perfect being who first made you and then bought you. Made in the image of God, then bought by the blood of God's dear Son, you are priceless.

I cannot say it often enough: You are worth it all.

And today is your turnaround day, the day when you step into your soul's true worth.

The Four Understandings of the Soul

Let me now walk you through the simple steps I have used in my life to shake off a sense of low self-worth and awaken myself to my true value. I promise you that these four steps will guide you to a healthier, more powerful, more life-giving soul.

1. Understand the value of your soul.
2. Understand soul shame.

3. Understand feelings of unworthiness.

4. Understand destructive thought patterns.

Step 1: Understand the value of your soul.

There are four components that determine the value of your soul:

◈ your soul's design
◈ your soul's designer
◈ your soul's durability
◈ your soul's demand

Let's break these four elements down.

◈ *Your soul is valuable because of its amazing design.* You might ask, "How is my soul designed?" I can tell you that it is designed in the image of God. As it says in Genesis 1:26: "Let us make man in our image, according to our likeness" (CSB). This means that the mark of the Creator is inside you. As it says in Psalm 139:13–14: "You formed my innermost being, shaping my delicate inside and my intricate outside, and wove them all together in my mother's womb. I thank you, God, for making me so mysteriously complex!" (TPT).

◈ *Your soul is valuable because of its heavenly designer.* You were not just made *like* God, you were also made *by* Him. Think about the astronomical price that people will pay for Jimmy Choo shoes, a Birkin bag or a Giorgio Armani suit. Is the price tag based on the cost of the materials used? Not entirely. You are also paying for the designer label. So think about it what is on the label of your soul: God. He is the greatest of all designers—the Creator of the universe, quite a lot bigger than Ralph Lauren and Calvin Klein. He went to great lengths to make you unique. No two people are alike, just as no two fingerprints are alike.

- *Your soul is valuable because of its durability.* Your soul has endured heartbreak, disappointment and discouragement. And yet you have made it through. Your soul has withstood physical disease and perhaps abuse from others. Still, you have survived. Your soul has also withstood torrents of negativity. And yet you are still standing. This all proves that your soul is durable. It has outlasted your enemies, outlasted your pain, outlasted your mistakes. Now you can make it through anything.

- *Your soul is in high demand.* Just like that Da Vinci painting, any product or artifact is worth what people will pay for it. And one of the things people will pay dearly for is rarity. But what is rarer than a human soul? There is only one of you in the universe. That is why your soul is in such high demand.

Let's think about that: Who or what is demanding your soul? The devil knows how valuable your soul is. But God knows how valuable you are, too.

That is why He was willing to sacrifice His Son to buy you back from sin. You might not be worth much to someone who treated you poorly, but to God, you are worth everything. "You were not redeemed with corruptible things, like silver or gold . . . but with the precious blood of Christ, as of a lamb without blemish and without spot" (1 Peter 1:18–19 NKJV).

Step 2: Understand soul shame.

We are all familiar with the paralysis of shame. Shame is the feeling that you are defective as a person, irreparably damaged. It is as if that little voice in your head is right after all—the one that says, *I knew you'd fail, You'll never really belong,* and *Who would love you?* You feel that if anyone really knew who you were on the inside, you would be rejected.

Shame also shows up as a painful feeling of humiliation. We feel as if we have done something foolish. We have made a dumb mistake that leaves us "shamefaced." At its most extreme, shame can even lead to suicide.

It is easy to see that this demonic emotion is the source of immense pain. It corrodes the very part of us that is capable of greatness, that believes we are worthy of receiving what we need from God.

- ◈ *Where did shame come from?* In Genesis 3:5–6, Satan convinced Eve that there was something wrong with her. As the passage about the fruit of the Tree of Life reads: "For God knows that when you eat of it your eyes will be opened, and you will be like God, knowing good and evil" (RSV). Notice that Eve did not sin because there was something wrong with her. She did it because she thought there was. We do not sin because we are evil. We sin because we are trying to fix something about ourselves that seems wrong or about which we are ashamed.

- ◈ *How do we heal shame?* The best way to heal shame is to remember that Jesus healed it for us on the cross. And that He certainly felt the full sting of shame as He hung helplessly on the cross. But because of His death, shame no longer has any rightful power over us. He nailed it to the cross with Him, and rose, leaving the shame buried forever in the depths of the sea. "You will cast all our sins into the depths of the sea" (Micah 7:19 NKJV).

As was foretold in Isaiah 53:3, "He was despised and rejected of men, a man of sorrows and acquainted with grief. And we hid, as it were, our faces from him; he was despised, and we did not esteem him" (MEV). And Paul, in his letter to the Hebrews, said of Jesus, "Because of the joy awaiting him, he endured the cross, disregarding its shame" (Hebrews 12:2 NLT). In his letter to the Romans, Paul wrote, "There is now no condemnation for those who are in Christ Jesus" (Romans 8:1 NIV).

Step 3: Understand feelings of unworthiness.

As you read this, you might yearn to receive what God has promised, which is unconditional love and acceptance. Yet there may be something inside you saying, *I don't deserve it. I'm not good enough. I haven't prayed long enough.* Our minds can come up with numerous justifications for self-crucifixion, right?

In other words, our persistent feelings of unworthiness cause us to object to or reject the favor that God has made available to us. Instead of holding our arms out and palms up, showing that we are ready to receive His blessings, we put our arms down and close our hands. That is the enemy at work in our lives, making us feel unworthy when we are the exact opposite.

We need to change our thinking and consider ourselves worth all the trouble God went through to make us, save us and bless us. Adjust your view of yourself by remembering God's Word every chance you get: "He found him in a desert land and in the wasteland, a howling wilderness; He encircled him, He instructed him, He kept him as the apple of His eye" (Deuteronomy 32:10 NKJV).

You are God's favorite child.

In other words, you are God's favorite child. You do not need to prove your worthiness to anyone. God has shown you how much you are worth by paying the ultimate price to bring you to Him. The Scripture says in Luke 19:10, "For the Son of Man has come to seek and to save that which was lost."

Step 4: Understand destructive thought patterns.

One way I have found to break destructive thought patterns is to play what I call the aim game (because each move rhymes with "aim"—that is how I can remember them). It is the opposite of the blame game, because this game is a process of aiming your thoughts in the *right* direction.

- ◈ *Name it.* Identify the thought that is making you suffer or feel "less than." Is it a thought of failure? Of powerlessness? Of mistakes? Of inferiority? Call it what it is. Do not defend or justify negative feelings about yourself. Call them out. Own them. (For more about this, see page 121.)

- ◆ *Frame it.* Put your situation in perspective. Nobody has it all together. So often we magnify our failures, our shortcomings. We make mountains out of molehills. We give our mistakes too much power. Instead, see a mistake for what it is. It is not the real you. You are bigger than your behavior. You are more valuable than the opinion others have of you.

- ◆ *Tame it.* Let's say I want to tame the emotion of anger. First I need to identify the thought that led to the anger. Then I need to put it in perspective: I perceived a slight to my rights. Someone cut me off on the highway, for example, and I got angry because I felt that he took over "my space" and that I had a "right" to the lane I was in. When I realize that it is not my highway and it is not my lane, I tame the destructive thought by telling myself, *I'm going to trust God to help me get where I'm going on time.* This is when anger loses its hold.

"Beloved, I pray that you may prosper in all things and be in health, just as your soul prospers" (3 John 2 NKJV).

Notice in this well-known verse that everything hinges on the health of the soul. And soul health starts with valuing yourself.

Whatever you value, you will take care of. When you buy a new car, you are meticulous with its care and cleanliness. But by the time you have had it a year or two, how often does the backseat or trunk end up as a hamper for dirty clothes or a magnet for old fast-food containers?

When you value yourself, you will regularly take out the mental trash, wiping your mind of all the negatives that weigh you down.

And that is why you must remember that no matter what happens in life, regardless of what you say or do, your intrinsic worth and value as a person never changes. Like that Da Vinci painting, you remain priceless.

The realization of your value is the foundation of everything great, of all your best decisions, habits and character. So get out your inner compass out and find true north, toward the route of worth and value. Remember that God is your Designer and you are His design—so much more precious than a Gucci bag or a Versace suit. He created your soul, which has everlasting durability.

The enemy of your soul has "demanded to have you, that he might sift you like wheat," as Jesus said, "but I have prayed for you that your faith may not fail" (Luke 22:31–32 ESV). And YOUR faith won't fail, because Jesus has also prayed for YOU.

The more firmly you believe that, the better care you will take of yourself. You will elevate your expectations because you have discovered your true worth. A well-taken-care-of soul is a soul that can reach its maximum potential, its highest purpose and its wildest dreams.

DECIDE AND DECLARE

◈ I am of great value and worth.
◈ I am a unique, rare, beautiful pearl of great price.
◈ I am cherished and wanted by my heavenly Father.
◈ The brokenness in my life will not diminish or tarnish my worth.
◈ My true worth is healing my soul and elevating my expectations.

NOW PRAY THIS WITH ME

Heavenly Father, I am grateful that in You I am cherished and wanted. I am twice Yours. First You made me with Your beautiful hands. Then You bought me with Jesus' outstretched hands. I am designed by You and designed like You, with durability that outlasts my pain, outlasts my enemies and outlasts my mistakes. Help me to find my true worth in You, so I may find healing for my soul and an elevation of my expectations. In Jesus' name, Amen.

PART II

BATTLING SOUL THIEVES

8

What Is Your Name?

Denial ain't just a river in Egypt.

Mark Twain

Over my thirty years of counseling people, I have noticed that it is often the simplest insight into our problems that will set us free. But like Watson, who sees only the stars (see page 25), we miss the obvious, though it is right in front of our eyes.

Let me illustrate it this way: One of my favorite miracles in the Bible is Jesus' encounter with a demon-possessed man in Luke 8:26–39. Jesus travels to the land of the Gerasenes, where he comes upon a diseased soul who is tormented and depressed, detached from any sense of value or purpose.

"What is your name?" Jesus asks the man.

Why would He ask something like that?

I had never heard a good answer to this question until this simple thought came to me one day: In order to cure or heal a condition and recover from it, you have to first name it, recognize it and acknowledge what it is.

But so often we do the opposite. Denial becomes a defense, an effort to cope with a situation by acting as if it does not exist or as if it is not happening. So we talk all around a problem, complaining about it, playing the victim, blaming others or ignoring it altogether.

When you refuse to name a weakness or pretend it is not there, it establishes a stronghold in your life, which can lead to depression, addiction and all forms of human misery.

Maybe you are in a relationship that is failing. Maybe you are in a work situation that has become intolerable. Maybe you are in financial debt or addicted to a behavior or substance that does not serve you.

But do not be afraid. We are not naming it or admitting to a problem in order to define us—or confine us.

You see, we are safe in the arms of God's nonjudgmental love and grace. We can freely fling open the door, the hinges of our heart, with absolute honesty and complete surrender. We can stand before God expectantly and wait for the winds of healing and waves of His love to overtake our souls and mend us everywhere we have ever been broken.

From the deepest to the widest to the darkest places of our heart, He will in no way cast us out. As Jesus said, "I will never reject them" (John 6:37 NLT). God knows it all. He forgives it all. And he is thrilled to heal it all. And for you, I believe that starts today.

So when Jesus asks, *What is your name?*, He is inviting you to call your problem what it is. Do not minimize it. Do not qualify it. Do not apologize for it. And do not explain it away. Just name it.

Are you struggling with anxiety? Name it. Are you dealing with depression or anger? Name it. Call it out. Face it. Do not *accept* it as it is, but *face* it as it is.

By naming it, you are attacking the things that have been attacking you for far too long.

So if we want to confront the condition of a broken soul and an unsettled mind, and if we want to truly be healed, we need look no further than this fascinating encounter that Jesus has in the land of the Gerasenes, where He sets a burdened man free.

In Luke 8:27, it says: "When [Jesus] stepped out on the land, there met Him a certain man from the city who had demons for a long time" (NKJV).

Notice that the devil loves to keep people in bondage for a long time, but Jesus loves to set people free.

Look at what the Bible says next: "And he wore no clothes, nor did he live in a house but in the tombs."

Naked and homeless, the diseased man lived among the dead.

A damaged soul affects every aspect of our existence—the quality of our living conditions, our physical health and our relationships. So the miracle that Jesus is about to perform is going to affect all three areas of life, demonstrating His dominion over the devil.

And if Jesus can do it, so can you. As He said in Luke 10:19, "Behold, I give you the authority to trample on serpents and scorpions, and over all the power of the enemy, and nothing shall by any means hurt you" (NKJV).

Isn't it true that we have been pushed around by the enemy of our souls for far too long, deceived into thinking he has more authority than we do? But God wants us to know that we have more authority than the devil. We just need to claim that power and learn how to walk in it.

It is all in Romans 5:17, where Paul explains that God has given us authority through "the abundance of grace and of the gift of righteousness." We reign in life.

Now, I know there are preachers out there who say, "Well, sometimes God heals and delivers, and sometimes He does not." But you are smarter than that. You know enough to believe the Bible instead of a preacher. After all, the Word of God explains itself.

But first we have to admit that we live in a fallen world. And we have to give a name to whatever it is that is afflicting us. Perhaps we were abused or bullied or damaged by a dysfunctional family life. Maybe we witnessed our parents scream at each other for hours on end. Sometimes something is done to us that hurts us. So we grow up with a pattern of brokenness.

The result? In adulthood, some people are susceptible to addictions—whether to alcohol, pornography or opioids. Still others are addicted to attention and approval. And some of us, like me, wound up with all those things—an all-in-one.

We have to give a name to whatever it is that is afflicting us.

I admit that I was a one-stop shop for soul thieves and demons! But when God saved me, it was as if He were saying, *Let me get my hands on this guy. Because if I get him saved and set free, people will believe anything is possible.* That is why I like to say, when God saved me, He saved the worst first.

As the Scripture says in Matthew 8:16, "That evening they brought to him many who were possessed with demons; and he cast out the spirits with a word, and healed all who were sick" (RSV). This passage shows Jesus' compassion for oppressed people, His commitment to seeing His work finished in the human soul and His fearlessness in the face of Satan and anything Satan can do.

How does this deliverance apply to us? Even though we may not have thousands of demons living inside of us, we do live in a fallen world, in dark "tombs" of our own, solitary places of torment. And we do have thousands of knives in our souls caused by what life has done to us, things inside that torture us.

So everybody has some personal demons. I'm not referring to demonic possession here, but rather our fears, insecurities and negative beliefs that are creating our suffering. These soul thieves poison us with worry and fear. And they haunt us with guilt about bad decisions we have made that have injured our lives.

The result? Our minds are filled with self-doubt, self-hatred and low self-worth. It is what I simply call a mentality of failure. These inner voices degrade us and weigh us down with their relentless negative chatter. They force us to compare and despair, so we never feel good enough. This leads to isolation, shame, guilt, worry, loneliness and depression.

It is as if we are the walking wounded, carrying around the scars of the past and the pain of our mistakes. Living this way does enormous damage to our vulnerable hearts, limiting our possibilities.

In this section of *Soul Cure*, we will tackle all these demons—these soul thieves—and remove them from our lives.

I can tell you that these enemy mindsets are contrary to God's view of us. And it is up to us to drive out these demonic parasites by flooding our soul with God's power and love. When we do that, it leaves no room for the devil. As it is written in James 4:7: "Therefore submit to God. Resist the devil and he will flee from you" (NKJV).

Remember, the devil can only ride the saddle of wrong thinking as long as we allow him to. Once we change saddles and push him off the horse, Satan cannot ride anymore. He has got to get off and get out of town, because, as they used to say in the Wild West, "This town ain't big enough for the two of us!"

But back to our story about Jesus in the land of the Gerasenes. Let's see what happens next.

"When [the afflicted man] saw Jesus, he cried out, fell down before Him, and with a loud voice said, 'What have I to do with You, Jesus, Son of the Most High God? I beg You, do not torment me!'" (Luke 8:28 NKJV).

The torment the man is speaking of is the eternal punishment of hell, where demons will ultimately be confined. But it also reminds us of the misconception of so-called religious people who believe that God is tormenting them or allowing some traumatic tragedy to take place in their lives, leaving them in a broken or lonely condition.

But why would Jesus torment anyone? You could only think this if you have a wrong view of God. When you meet the real Jesus, the thought that He could torment you will never cross your mind. He would never put sickness or trouble in your life.

We know that everywhere Jesus went, He lifted burdens. He loved the unlovable. He fed the hungry. He had mercy on the sinner and compassion for the suffering. He healed the sick, raised the dead, cleansed the lepers and cast out demons.

117

The only people He tormented were self-righteous, religious people who prided themselves on appearing superior to others. He tormented their religion because their religion tormented people. And Jesus loves to set people free.

Freedom from Loneliness and Solitary Places

Back to our story: Jesus brings healing to the afflicted man, commanding that the evil spirits be cast out from him, and with them all the loneliness and oppression they brought. Let's look at Luke 8:29: "For Jesus had commanded the demonic spirit to come out of the man. Many times it had seized him, and though he was chained hand and foot and kept under guard, he had broken his chains and had been driven by the demon into *solitary places*" (NIV, emphasis added).

The concept of solitary places is particularly relevant to our world today. It reveals how Satan operates in people's lives, feeding alienation and isolation, which often leads to self-hurt and violent impulses.

This corruption of the soul is where fear is born, spawning self-hate and a devaluation of self and others. I believe that this evil of the soul originates from the wounds of rejection (the activity of the evil one), driving people into solitary places.

Satan is trying to drive people to solitary places because that is where they remain abused. That is where they remain broken by the environment in which they grew up. That is where they remain lonely. That is where they become loners. That is where they have no one to challenge the voices in their head that are telling them to hurt themselves or someone else. Solitary places of the soul are the wombs of anxiety, insecurity, violence and fear.

But these are not the only casualties of isolation. Perhaps you have a friend or a loved one who has been consumed by an addiction or some other form of self-injury. It usually happens because that person has been driven into a solitary, lonely place in his or her soul. And loneliness can be a killer.

In fact, a person who commits a crime of hate is usually a loner. But God's love can set the lonely free. As the Bible says in Psalm 68:6: "God sets the lonely in families" (NIV); "he brings out those who are bound with chains" (JUB).

We have to break those chains of loneliness, which is why God created a supernatural force on this earth that is permeated with a culture of hope and family (aka the Church). And He encourages all of us to be connected to a healthy one, because that is where healing happens. On a daily basis, we need the Word of God and the family of God to counteract Satan's intent to drive us into solitary places, where we are deprived of the strength we need to encourage us forward.

That is the first way we can show practical love and practice powerful spiritual warfare—by reaching out to the lonely ones around us. Break through their isolation. Start by just saying hi to them. Let's not let the current societal dividers keep us divided from the people we are put on this earth to serve and help.

I was a loner in junior high and high school, withdrawn and depressed. By the age of sixteen, I was an alcoholic and addicted to drugs. This left me in an emotional place of isolation, a solitary place in my soul.

I was not someone who would share what I was going through, and I certainly would not let anybody in. Instead, I was guarded, pretending to be invulnerable. Like many of us, I had a secret self—hiding in my shell. Some called it shy; at the time, I just called it me.

I was also fighting the social anxiety cycle of self-consciousness—the overwhelming sensation of feeling observed but not approved. We all are observed at various times in life, and we get used to it. But to be observed without feeling approved is a scary feeling that took me to that solitary, lonely place in my soul.

In short, my soul was so depressed and discouraged that I let nobody into it. I guarded it. I protected it. What I am trying to say is that the best thing that ever happened to me was when somebody busted through that solitary confinement and said, "Hey, man, how you doing? Want to come to Bible study with me?"

Somebody cared. Somebody reached out. Who knows what I would have become years later if nobody would have reached out? I could have gone even deeper into darkness. But that simple act of love and compassion made all the difference.

And today, you can do the same thing. Reach out to that loner—that person at work, that person in your family, that person in your neighborhood or school who is in pain. You can make a difference. Do not be afraid to reach out. Love never fails. This kind of love will break down walls and crack open that shell of loneliness. Love will cast out fear.

Otherwise, we know what happens when people are left to themselves in a "solitary" place—they are overcome by the inner voices of rejection and fear.

That is why Scripture says that one can put a thousand to flight and two can put ten thousand to flight (see Deuteronomy 32:30).

That is why Scripture says that when you are planted in the house of God you will flourish (see Psalm 92:13).

That is why Jesus said that where two or three of us are gathered in His name He will be in the midst of us (see Matthew 18:20).

And that if two people shall agree about anything they ask it shall be done by God (see verse 19).

In short, there is deliverance, there is freedom, and there is a healing through the power of connection—the right kind of connection, that is.

Clothed and in Your Right Mind

Let's continue to watch the healing of the man from the land of the Gerasenes unfold, and in doing so, unlock the secret to our own healing.

As we saw, in Luke 8:30, the first thing Jesus said to the man is, "What is your name?"

The man replies, "Legion," referring to the six thousand demons living inside him.

The good news is he named his condition. Likewise, we have to name the thing we are struggling with. Why? Because only when you call it out, can you be set free from it. When a problem has a name, the one who is called "the name above all names" (Philippians 2:9 BSB) will deliver you from it.

When you name it, you are being honest about it. When you name it, you are opening your soul to let Jesus deliver you from it and heal you from it.

> When a problem has a name, the one who is called "the name above all names" will deliver you from it.

When we refuse to admit a weakness, hide from it or simply pretend that we are dealing with it, we remain stuck in it. And that is where it remains. It defeats us from within. In fact, because it operates in solitary places, it gets an even stronger hold on our lives. But that can all change.

Now to the climax of the story, in Luke 8:32–37.

> A herd of many swine was feeding there on the mountain. So they begged Him that He would permit them to enter them. And He permitted them. Then the demons went out of the man and entered the swine, and the herd ran violently down the steep place into the lake and drowned.
>
> When those who fed them saw what had happened, they fled and told it in the city and in the country. Then they went out to see what had happened, and came to Jesus, and found the man from whom the demons had departed, sitting at the feet of Jesus, clothed and in his right mind. And they were afraid. They also who had seen it told them by what means he who had been demon-possessed was healed. Then the whole multitude of the surrounding region of the Gadarenes asked Him to depart from them, for they were seized with great fear. And He got into the boat and returned. (NKJV)

Those who had known the demon-possessed man were more afraid of him after he had been healed than before. When the man was living among the dead, when he was breaking chains, when he was cutting himself with stones, when he was gnashing his teeth, and when he was crying out, yelling and screaming, nobody was afraid. They dismissed him.

But when the man sat at the feet of Jesus—clothed, in his right mind—people freaked out. We have to stop getting used to things being abnormal.

When I was lonely and addicted, none of my friends seemed too concerned. (If they were, I was unaware of it.) But after I got saved, they asked, "What's wrong with Greg?"

Now I was not doing drugs anymore. Now I was not selling drugs anymore. But still, my friends asked, "What happened to Greg? We need to get him some help."

Thank God that Jesus is my helper, and that is where my help comes from. Praise God! I am just glad Jesus saved me. He is still working on me, too. (Aren't you glad about that? 😄)

Now, notice verse 35: "They . . . came to Jesus, and found the man from whom the demons had departed, sitting at the feet of Jesus, clothed and in his right mind."

This is really key, for no longer was that demon-possessed man naked and out of his mind. The demons had been dealt with by Jesus. But although the deliverance of this man was instantaneous, transformation in most people is a process. It does not happen right away. Stick to the process, and you will end up with the progress. So let's slow the movie down a little bit and take a closer look.

> Stick to the process, and you will end up with the progress.

As we follow the road map to emotional health and healing as laid out in this book so far, and in the chapters to follow, several things are going to begin to show up in our lives.

What does it mean to be in your right mind?

A right mind will make "right" decisions, experience "right" emotions and create "right" living.

But you cannot manufacture emotional wellness. And so often, religious traditions and rituals put the cart before the horse, imposing a predetermined version of living "right" from the outside in. It falsely promises, *Do this, don't do that, and it will lead to a righteous life.* But that is a recipe for misery and failure.

We need to experience it from the inside out. Otherwise, we end up back where we started, stuck in the old pattern, where nothing changes. But when we confront our demons, attacking the things that have been attacking us internally, we will begin to come into our right mind (right mind = right direction).

So first we name the thing afflicting or addicting us. Then we attack it with all the ammunition Jesus has given us, using all the tools in this book. This process includes discovering our worth, being swept away by God's relentless love, experiencing radical forgiveness and discovering the most powerful words on earth (*thank you*), all of which will go to work on every damaged part of our souls. And all this healing is found simply by sitting at the feet of Jesus, just as we witnessed with the formerly demon-possessed man. If he could be healed, anyone can.

Sitting at the feet of Jesus also means leaning in and listening. Sometimes I think we spend too much of our time wanting God to listen to *us* as we whine and pout and pour out all the things we want and list the people we want Him to wipe off the face of the earth. Ha! But we really need to learn to listen. That is why He gave us one mouth and two ears—so we can listen twice as much as we speak.

It reminds me of the story of the cowboy riding his horse, when he suddenly came upon a man lying flat on the ground with his ear pressed to the earth. The man struggled but was able to say, "Wagon. One mile off. One man. Two horses. One gray. One brown. One man in a red flannel shirt."

The cowboy was so impressed, he said, "How amazing. You can tell all that just by listening to the earth?"

The man sighed. "No, idiot. They ran over me thirty minutes ago. Go after them!"

Well, you get the point. We need to keep our ears to the "ground" so to speak, listening with expectation for God's still, small voice (1 Kings 19:12).

The pages that follow, about battling soul thieves, are designed to give you a space to hear God's loving voice. You are going to sit and take a rest.

Remember, you have a seat at God's table. You do not have to compete with others for that seat. God has reserved it just for you. Yet so often we feel as if we have to fight or compete for that seat or try to prove we are special or significant enough to get it. But you do not have to.

Know this: You have VIP seating anytime you choose. There is an amazing verse in Scripture, Ephesians 2:6, that says God has "raised us up with Christ and seated us with him in the heavenly realms" (NIV).

In my own life, when I finally embraced this truth and realized that God had given me my own seat at the table, equal to anyone else's, I felt a jolt of confidence, a feeling that I had arrived. I was not a finished product, but I felt secure in the absolute assurance that I had a seat at the table.

All that I longed for—belonging, recognition and a sense of significance—was mine, because God had placed me at His table. And you are there as well, sitting at the feet of Jesus, clothed and in your right mind.

> You are not your problem. You are not your struggle.

With that knowledge inside you, do not be afraid to name your soul thieves. *You* are not your problem. *You* are not your struggle. Naming something does not strap you to that label; rather, it opens you up for the healing power of God to come rushing in.

You are safe in the arms of God.

His love will heal us everywhere we have ever been broken. But this can only happen when you are in a state of vulnerability and surrender. So when Jesus asks, *What is your name?*, He is conveying a profound message.

And while I have done my very best to explain why Jesus would ask this question, I will drop this additional nugget into your soul: By asking the possessed man's name, Jesus preserved the man's dignity. Even though he was unrecognizable after demons had ravaged his soul and body, Jesus saw his true worth. By asking his name, He showed empathy, interest and respect. By asking his name, Jesus shows us that none of us is just a face in the crowd, battling our soul thieves by ourselves. We are real individual human beings whom God is deeply interested in getting to know. He wants to know each of us on a first-name basis, in an intimate way, restoring our sense of value and worth.

What is your name? You are loved. You are accepted. You are significant. You are enough. You are *you*.

Decide and Declare

◈ I am free from every chain that has kept me isolated and lonely.

◈ I am free from all abuse, including self-abuse and self-hate.

◈ I reject the labels that have defined me and confined me.

◈ I am loved.

◈ I am accepted.

◈ I am significant.

◈ I am enough.

Now Pray This with Me

Today I choose to rest by sitting at Your feet, Jesus. May Your grace and goodness work in my soul. You know me by name. I am safe in Your loving arms. Thank You for setting me free from the demons and thieves that have been at work in my soul and from labels that have defined me and confined me—they had me trapped and immobilized, but they no longer do. I am so grateful that You are restoring me to the dignity, health and abundance that You created me for, Amen.

9

Let No One Take Your Crown

I am coming quickly; hold firmly to what you have, so that
no one will take your crown.

Revelation 3:11

He had just turned 85 years old.

Not usually a good age to take on the battle of one's life.

Most people would just be happy to be alive and well at that age. To settle for mere existence. But Caleb was not most people.

He had waited all his life for this. He had prepared for such a time as this. He was ready to do the impossible.

As others complained and others feared and others doubted, he took charge: "Caleb tried to quiet the people as they stood before Moses. 'Let's go at once to take the land,' he said. 'We can certainly conquer it!'" (Numbers 13:30 NLT).

Now, you probably remember the rest of the story. Moses had just sent twelve men to check out the Promised Land, to see if it was a land worth conquering. Ten of these men trembled. Two of the men believed.

What was the difference?

Caleb and Joshua knew they could take the land of the giants. The other ten men did not. It has been said that if you think you can or if you think you cannot, you are right.

The ten men said, "We were like grasshoppers in our own sight, and so we were in their sight" (Numbers 13:33 NKJV).

Notice that everybody saw the same giants. Everybody perceived the giants as big. It was the way they perceived *themselves* that made the difference.

No matter what the other ten spies said or thought, Caleb and Joshua just were not gonna let anyone rob them of the victory they knew God had in store for them.

That brings me to something Jesus said in Revelation 3:11: "I am coming soon. Hold on to what you have, so that no one will take your crown" (NIV).

"So that no one will take your crown" implies that we actually have a crown. Otherwise, Jesus would not have told us to let no one take it.

The Crown of God's Creation

As God's Word says in Psalm 8:5–6, "You have crowned [mankind] with glory and honor. You have made him to have dominion over the works of Your hands; You have put all things under his feet" (NKJV).

Let's think about that. God has given us a crown of glory, an amazing symbol of royalty, usually worn by a monarch as a symbol of authority. This is telling us something significant. A crown sits on your head, which has inside it the miracle of your brain, the home of what you think, along with all your emotions and the power of your will.

Our thinking needs to be permeated by this "crown" mindset. We need to know that God gave us the crown and what it represents. It should be the lens through which the rest of life is viewed.

It could also be called a victor's attitude. As I said earlier, an attitude is a mindset that takes precedence over all other facts. So no matter what's going on in your life, your mindset needs to remain fixed on this crowned condition. You have to see yourself as ruling and reigning rather than whining and complaining. You are a winner. More than a winner. You have been crowned. Yes, the crown that I speak of is a victor's crown, but it is so much more than that. It is an attitude or mindset of royalty.

Each of us deserves to feel not only worthy but also royal, crowned by God's love and imprinted with His seal of approval.

He made you. He loves you. And He crowned you, giving you an amazing "head" start.

That crown is His blessing, the gift of greatness just for being one of His kids. That is why Jesus told us to let no one take our crown.

People are going to try to take it from you. Discouraging moments are going to try to take it from you. Mistreatment and discrimination are going to try to take it from you. Your guilt over past mistakes is going to try to take it from you. And the devil is going to try to take it from you. But let *no one* and *nothing* take your crown.

Royalty Destroys Inferiority

Along the way on my journey, I heard a game-changing statement that I have been saying over and over ever since. And it is simply this: Royalty destroys inferiority.

We all know that a king is inferior to no one in his land. And Jesus is the King of kings.

He knew who He was and lived His life with no sense of inferiority, no insecurity. And Revelation 1:6 declares that Jesus, through His precious blood, "has made us kings and priests unto God and his Father" (JUB).

> We are part of the royal bloodline. We are heirs of all God's promises.

So there it is. We are in the royal family. We are part of the royal bloodline. We are heirs of all God's promises. Our heavenly Father's inheritance is ours. He said so.

But let's go a little deeper.

129

Why do people feel inferior? Why is it so easy to knock the crowns off our heads?

Certainly negative childhood experiences play a huge role. Rejection by significant others is traumatic. Being unduly criticized can be life-altering. And as we grow, taking others' opinions too much to heart can send us into a spiral of second-guessing, condemning and even hating ourselves.

And as we reach adulthood, everything from physical disease and aging to financial uncertainty and relationship problems conspires to capitalize on the inferiority complex we got saddled with, making us feel small and afraid. The things we were designed by God to have dominion over actually have dominion over us.

In this state, to feel "bigger," we sometimes act out in a variety of ways. Some of us revert to criticism of others. "Sure, she might look good, but I wonder how much plastic surgery she's had." Ouch!

Some of us overcompensate by boasting or projecting an exaggerated appearance of success or power, jealously competing with others who intimidate us. You'll see that dynamic operating in any playground bully or insecure boss.

A gentleman I know in his fifties is balding and getting a bit of a belly. He feels inferior and no longer wants to be seen in any situation that intimidates him or puts him in competition with people younger than he is. It is not his age or hair loss that is holding him back. It is his preexisting negative view of himself.

Others who feel inferior may aim to control the people around them, though God never intended any man or woman to dominate another. But in our mistaken crisis of identity, we do this often. So while it is actually God's will for us to *serve* one another, we often initiate a power struggle instead.

And there are many other facets to inferiority: Some of us experience intense performance anxiety; some crave attention and become aggressive; some try to manipulate people emotionally or financially; many become especially sensitive to criticism and feel easily disrespected in any situation (hence the epidemic of road rage, domestic violence, and spousal and child abuse).

Finally, when riddled with insecurity, we become selfish—obsessed about how we look, what we have and how we compare to others. This puts us into bondage, entrapped by a view of ourselves as small. We see others as a threat rather than as a brother, sister or friend.

But regardless of how inferiority is felt or expressed, nobody wants to feel it, right?

So what is the answer? How do we stop this cycle and break the back of this curse of inferiority? Well, here is a start: Discover the crown that Jesus gave you. Wear it.

When you fall or get pushed around by life, get up and straighten that crown on your head. When someone tries to belittle you, get up, keep your crown on and walk out of the room.

With this crown on—a victory mentality—our thinking is elevated, our vision is lifted and we break barriers that we never thought we could break. Keep in mind that as a man "thinks in his heart, so is he" (Proverbs 23:7 NKJV). Royalty thinking leads to royalty living.

Royalty thinking leads to royalty living.

An understanding of our bloodline as a new creation in Christ fosters a victor's attitude and a positive mindset that reflect our royal heritage. When we embrace a royal-bloodline point of view, we adopt a victorious, conquering mindset. No matter what's going on in life, with this attitude of royalty, you will think like a winner and prevail over any challenge.

It is simple: Royalty destroys inferiority.

Contrast the 85-year-old Caleb I wrote about at the opening of this chapter with a woman named Mary.

She was beautiful to everyone—except herself. She felt she was "not enough." In her mind, her figure was not slim enough, the men she had been with were not kind enough, her accomplishments were not significant enough . . . you get the idea. Nothing was enough.

Like millions of others, she had an inferior view of herself that was reflected in her life choices. Hers is an extreme situation. But God shows us what can happen to anyone overtaken by self-hate, intimidation and inferiority. Mary went on to sell herself piece by piece until there was nothing left in her that felt whole. That is, until something happened.

She met a man. She met *the* man. She met the Son of Man. Jesus valued her. Jesus elevated her. Jesus saw her worth, just as He sees yours. Jesus gave her a crown. With that crown of forgiveness and worth in and on her head, she found hope. She took a new breath. She caught a true glimpse of her beauty from the inside out. She was changed forever. She poured out her love on Jesus for forgiving her and restoring to her a crown of royalty as a daughter of God.

What a snapshot into the heart of God and His love for His children.

The root of inferiority that insidiously poisons the soul of humanity dates back to Adam and Eve, once clothed with dominion over the earth and the glory of God. They lost it all when they believed the lie that they were not enough.

"Go ahead and eat from that tree that God told you not to eat from," the devil said. "God is just holding out on you. You'll be *more* if you do it your way."

The problem was, there was no "more" after God had already created Adam and Eve in His own image. They were already enough. They just stopped believing it. And they fell from God's glory.

It reminds me of Romans 3:23: "All have sinned and fall short of the glory of God" (NIV). The word *glory* here means "to become all that God intended you to be." The term *short of* means "to be inferior."

So the Scripture is saying that because of sin, we became inferior to all that God intended us to be. Sin brought the curse of inferiority. And we have all been there. But Jesus cured all that when He died for our sin and made us new creatures in Him.

But the curse of inferiority opens wide the floodgates of its offspring: insecurity, jealousy, pride, resentment, domination, subjugation, false superiority and racism—to name just a few. They are all ways of compensating for the plague of inferiority that afflicts us.

But in our battle with inferiority, we often attempt to dominate or manipulate or control another person. In fact, in our efforts to compensate for our sense of inadequacy and unworthiness, we cover ourselves with the fig leaves of false superiority. We do this to gain ascendency over others, believing it will make us feel better about ourselves.

Nations do it, too. Just think back to the infancy of America, a sad history of white dominance over the black race, enslaving and stigmatizing an entire people for financial and emotional gain. The payoff was centuries of damage, which we are still trying to undo today.

The same thread of evil, hauntingly, surfaced two centuries later, when Hitler attempted to dominate the world, trying to elevate the "Aryan" race by killing millions of people, all to feed his false sense of superiority. Likewise, Mao Zedong killed millions of his Chinese countrymen to gain power over a ruthlessly bullied population.

All these hideous marks on history—slavery, fascism, dictatorships—reveal the fallen nature of humankind.

Contemporary history is no better. Think about the terrorists of 9/11, who perpetrated evil on America, believing their cause was holy. Not to mention the stratospheric rise in mass shootings and terrorist attacks worldwide and the racial tensions that still seem to linger and carry on.

So why is there still such hatred and violence in the world? No doubt it is because people are still in bondage to a sense of inferiority, which often is only alleviated by a false sense of superiority. Why else would someone think of himself as better than somebody else? Such people feel weak and insecure, unable to tolerate any perceived threats to their already fragile egos.

Back to the Garden of Eden for a moment: Having fallen short of God's intention, Adam and Eve felt rejected, exposed, naked and ashamed. And their natural inclination (as is ours) was to cover over that inferiority. Fast-forward: Every negative emotion we feel today, every impulse we have to dominate or subjugate others, is rooted in the same sense of powerlessness, rooted in the same sense of inferiority.

Victims No More

How do we turn it around? As Paul wrote in Romans 11:16, "If the root is holy, the branches are as well." In other words, the branches of inferiority in life come from a root system that must be cut off.

And that root system is your belief system. Your healing begins in your thinking. Each of us has around 65,000 thoughts a day—often exactly the same negative ones as we had the day before. We need to start telling ourselves a new story about our worth, our royalty and our God-given rights. "I *can* be healed. I am victorious. I am more than a conqueror."

> Your healing begins in your thinking.

So shift your thinking and it will lift your life. Be confident in God's love and who He says you are. Straighten that crown that life keeps trying to knock off of your head. Stop telling a sob story to yourself and blaming others for your condition. You have the power to change it.

Do what Jesus said so many times to so many people: Rise and "walk." No, you don't have to "run," figuratively, or have it all figured out. Life is a marathon, not a sprint. But in order to claim your true worth and fulfill your true potential, you just need to take the next step forward. By doing that, you become the owner of your own life.

There are, of course, many negative forces that attempt to knock off our crown and erase our royal mindset. I cannot tell you how many people have come to me, telling stories about parents or teachers who belittled them with criticism or limiting narratives, such as

◈ *You are not smart enough to get in that college; you should settle for something less ambitious.*

* *You are not pretty enough to be a model or an actress; try something more practical.*
* *You will never be able to own your own business, so you better get used to working for someone else.*

On and on.

But nobody should be defined by such false prophecies. We must rule over the kingdom of our minds and realize that we are in control of our own lives. As Eleanor Roosevelt wisely said, "No one can make you feel inferior without your permission."[1]

I love that. You see, it all starts in your thinking, your view of yourself.

Sure, at some point in life, whether as children, teenagers or adults, we have all felt victimized. Some more than others. But we have all suffered some kind of emotional or physical pain.

But we do not have to be defined by it, justifying our unhappiness by blaming it on the past. In fact, nurturing that victim mentality forces us to view our entire existence through a very narrow lens. We end up living with the expectation of the next negative thing to control our lives.

> "In all these things we are more than conquerors through Him who loved us."

In Genesis 4, Cain felt like a victim, too, perceiving that God respected his brother, Abel, but not him. So he thought, *I'll get rid of my brother, and these feelings will go away.* But by killing Abel, he only further imprisoned himself within a cage of inferiority and isolation.

His sense of inferiority reduced him to a jealous, bitter life. He ended up wandering in the wilderness the rest of his life.

We, by contrast, do not have to play the victim. As Paul wrote in Romans 8:37, "In all these things we are more than conquerors through Him who loved us" (MEV).

We are the victors. We are the champions, my friends! We are more than conquerors. We can throw off the mentality of failure that leads us to make bad decisions that damage ourselves and others.

Let no one take your crown.

Let's silence the voices that are trying to tell us,

- *You're not strong enough to break free from your past.*
- *You can't recover from this addiction.*
- *You can't bounce back from the financial mess you've made.*
- *It's going to be tough to get a new job. You're too damaged, too broken, too far gone, too old.*

No, no, no!

These tired broken records are lies sown in our heart by the evil one, urging us to give up on ourselves. They are the voices that get inside our heads, trying to keep us down. But we need to silence those voices by making our own sounds—by declaring the precious truth that we are wonderfully made by God, chosen and appointed, empowered and anointed.

In short, our destiny is greater than our history. Let's refuse to let history drive us backward. Instead, let's seize our destiny, one thought at a time. One voice at a time.

Let *no one* take your crown.

Embrace your mantle as a son or daughter of God. Assume your place and your power—the power to forgive, to dream, to achieve and to get up when you have fallen.

So if you ever feel defeated, like you cannot make it, or like you have reached your limit, that is the moment to stop and remember: You have been crowned with royalty as God's son or daughter.

Oh, I know, you may hear condemning voices in your head saying you are not worthy or deserving, voices attempting to browbeat you with mistaken beliefs and lies.

But you need to talk back to that inferiority complex with royal utterance: "No, you are not taking my crown. I am a child of the King. I am the head, not the tail. I am more than enough. And I believe that God is the God of breakthroughs. So I will break out of my limitations, because I have royal DNA running through my veins."

Remember, God did not crown you because you are deserving. He did it because you are in the royal family of heaven through the blood of Jesus.

Knowing that, you still might ask: *If I have this crown, why am I constantly getting conquered? Why do I feel victimized by the things that happen in life?*

The answer is that the concept of royalty has not yet permeated your head, where the crown must rule. That is where all positive perceptions of identity are cultivated.

Read the Scriptures about your destiny—to reign with a crown mindset rather than be ruled by its insecure fears. Think on these great promises and embrace them as your own.

◈ Deuteronomy 28:13: "The LORD will make you the head, not the tail" (NIV).

◈ Ephesians 2:6: "And God raised us up with Christ and seated us with him in the heavenly realms" (NIV).

◈ Psalm 103:2, 4: "Bless the LORD . . . who redeems your life from the pit, who crowns you with lovingkindness and tender mercies" (MEV).

◈ Isaiah 62:3: "You shall be a crown of beauty in the hand of the LORD" (ESV).

◈ Romans 5:17—my favorite: "Those who receive the abundance of grace and of the *gift of righteousness* reign in life through the One, Jesus Christ" (emphasis added).

Case closed. You are the son or daughter of the King, and that must permeate your mind day in and day out.

Pay special attention to the words "gift of righteousness" in Romans 5:17. What is this gift? Righteousness is the ability to stand in the presence of God without a sense of guilt, inferiority or condemnation.

You stand there as if sin had never been. That is how Adam and Eve stood with God before they sinned, before they became emotionally ruled people. There was no inferiority complex. There was no sense of guilt or shame. There was no discouragement or depression. They were on top of the world.

And though we sin, everything was restored to us when Jesus, who knew no sin, gave us, through his suffering, the righteousness of God. If you are born again, you, too, have it within you. You, too, are standing right with God. He is proud of you.

Royal, Not High and Mighty

In our mission to claim our crown and recover from inferiority, we cannot get self-righteous.

The opposite of inferiority is not superiority but royalty—a sense of truly knowing who you are and what you are entitled to as a child of God. It is a healthy sense of freedom and our royal rights, the cure for feeling inferior.

But at the same time, we must maintain a humble attitude about ourselves and embrace only what God says about us. Keep in mind that you did not crown yourself. God crowned you. Yes God crowned *you*.

And so only He has the authority to take it away. But he will never do that. As the Scripture says in Romans 11:29, "God's gifts and his call are irrevocable" (NIV).

So often we allow ourselves to be browbeaten by religious notions that tell us we are lowly, inferior creatures who should just be grateful that we will make it into heaven. This "settle-for-little" mentality leads to a negative view of ourselves and others.

But the real Jesus longs for you to discover your worth, your royal position as a child of God. He did not die for trash. He died for what he treasured: you.

As it says in Revelation 1:5–6, "To Him who loved us and washed us from our sins in His own blood, and made us kings and priests, to Him be glory and dominion" (NKJV).

Notice the three things it says that God did for us.

First He loved us. Then He washed us. Then He made us kings and priests. You are made a king. Jesus is the King of kings. And you and I are the kings that He is King of! He transformed us from slaves, ruled by sin, into something royal, ruled by His love. Knowing this is liberating, life-changing and even world-changing.

> He transformed us from slaves, ruled by sin, into something royal, ruled by His love.

Once you know this, no longer will you think of yourself as an inferior creature who has to grovel before God for a morsel of bread in your time of need. You will no longer be a victim of mistaken identity. Instead, you will take your power of permission back.

Declare today: "I refuse to give anyone permission to make me feel inferior. I will no longer be dominated by my past, weaknesses, fears and limitations. No longer will I allow my mistakes to sabotage me or disqualify me from that crown of royalty. After all, God knew about my mistakes before I made them, and He still chose to crown me with glory, not shame."

Simply put, no matter what your troubles, fears, broken pieces and mental limitations are, you no longer have to give in to feeling oppressed, overpowered, or dominated.

To oppress someone is to remove that person's power to control his or her own future. But you are taking your future back by refusing to let anyone take your crown. You have moved from Loser Lane to Conquerors Court. And you are a masterpiece in process. God's "got" you. He is working on you. And He will always finish what He started in you (see Philippians 1:6).

So the next time a voice tells you that you will never recover from what has been lost or burned in your life, reject it. Silence it with God's promise in Joel 2:25: "I will restore to you the years that the locust swarm devoured" (ISV).

And the next time you find yourself gripped with a people-pleasing mentality, giving others permission to make you feel inferior, let that go, too. Just straighten that crown on your head and remember who you are. A son or daughter of God. More than a conqueror.

Be aware of the barrage of self-doubt waiting for you on social media as well. Keep your guard up. You will be tempted to compare and despair. Focus on the person God made you to be. Focus on what He says about you. Whatever you focus on is what you will eventually feel.

We all appreciate moral support, but let's lose interest in how many "likes" others give us when we engage online. Instead, let's focus on giving "likes" to ourselves. Let's free ourselves from dependence on digital stamps of approval and the opinions of others.

Jesus said in John 5:41, "Your approval or disapproval means nothing to me" (TLB). Wow, what freedom! And this freedom is yours. You have God's approval. You have been given a crown of glory and royalty. Take your freedom back. Take your confidence back. And let no one take your crown.

Steps to Coronation

So how do we release ourselves from mental bondage and attain a sense of confident royalty? By doing the following.

- ◈ Realize that you were God's idea; He created you.
- ◈ Embrace His stamp of approval.
- ◈ Do not feel bad about being yourself, about being different, or about having weaknesses. We all have them. Let's stop letting them have us.

Fortified with God's stamp of approval, no longer will you cave in to self-consciousness or self-degradation. You will see that you do not need the "correct" looks, job, income or personality to be acceptable.

God already approves of you. That is not to say we should be irresponsible or reckless with our choices and behaviors. We should walk in faith and wisdom. But first and foremost, focus on God's approval in the depth of your soul. Embrace it. And approve of yourself.

Wear the crown you have been given by God. And do not let anyone take it away from you. Your life will take on a whole new meaning and direction when you do. Remember, His righteousness is the greatest gift we can possibly receive when we are born again. Romans 5:17 says it best: "Those who receive the abundance of grace and of the gift of righteousness reign in life through the One, Jesus Christ."

When we accept it, we restore our superiority—NOT OVER PEOPLE, but over sin, sickness, fear, anxiety, depression and discouragement; over every negative emotion and circumstance we will ever face. Make up your mind not to settle for a life below your privileges as a son or daughter of the King of kings. Your perception of yourself will create the reality you live in.

So straighten your crown right now. Shake off the lies and false beliefs that are robbing you of blessings of peace and abundance. And rise!

As it is written in Luke 21:19, "By your patience possess your souls" (NKJV). As I see it, if we do not possess our own souls, something or someone else will. So how do we do that?

1. Discover your power.

All negative emotions come from a sense of powerlessness, but Jesus rescues and delivers us from the oppression of victimhood and inferiority. So no longer can we play the victim.

2. Change your perspective.

Stop thinking life is happening *to* you and start believing that it is happening *for* you. As I said ealier, practice gratitude, which chemically activates happiness in your brain.

3. Identify your mistaken beliefs.

Most suffering in life is the result of misperceptions about ourselves. And all suffering originates in beliefs that go unquestioned. These mistaken beliefs create anxiety, depression, anger and blame. But when you know that God is for you, not against you, these false notions lose their power and are replaced with positive thoughts that improve soul health.

4. Understand your rights.

You were created by God to be free—liberated from your past, your pain and your suffering. That is your inalienable right. But when you feel like your freedom is taken away, the resulting powerlessness leads to anger and depression. No matter where you live, none of the rights granted to you by your government can compare to the rights you have as a king and priest of God's creation. What are those rights? Below are a few.

- ◈ You have the right to go to the throne of God and ask for His help at any time (see Hebrews 4:16).
- ◈ You have the right to forgive yourself and others, as Jesus forgave you (see Colossians 3:13).
- ◈ You have the right to be healed (see Matthew 15:28).
- ◈ You have the right to get back up when you have fallen (see Proverbs 24:16)
- ◈ You have the right to pray with confidence (see 1 John 3:21).
- ◈ You have the right to speak to life's mountains and command them to move (see Matthew 17:20)

Yes, you have been crowned with royalty, victory and power.

So do not let anyone take this crown by misleading you with a watered-down version of your blood-bought rights as a child of God.

DECIDE AND DECLARE

◆ I am a child of the King.

◆ No one is taking my crown—I am entitled to it.

◆ I refuse to give anyone permission to make me feel inferior.

◆ I am now free from my past.

◆ My weaknesses, fears and limitations no longer define me.

◆ I am the head, not the tail.

◆ I am more than enough.

NOW PRAY THIS WITH ME

Jesus, thanks to You, I will no longer be dominated by my past—or by my weaknesses, fears and limitations. No longer will I allow my mistakes to sabotage me or disqualify me from the crown of royalty that You have given me. After all, You knew about my mistakes before I made them, and You still chose to crown me with glory, not shame. And I believe that You are the God of breakthroughs. So I will break out of my limitations, because I have royal DNA running through my veins. Through Your abundance of grace and Your gift of righteousness, I reign in life, Amen.

10

Depressed No More

I have told you this so that my joy may be in you and that
your joy may be complete.

John 15:11 NIV

As I sat down to write this chapter about dealing a deathblow
to depression, I actually felt a momentary wave of depression suddenly—but not surprisingly—sweep over my soul.
It was not new to me, because I had felt it many times before. It
was that familiar feeling of exhaustion mixed with a sense of being
overwhelmed, with a bit of discouragement sprinkled on top.

We have all felt that. Haven't we? Some more than others. But I have
been acquainted with that feeling most of my life. And I have fought
it off many, many times over the years.

This time I heard God's voice reminding me of something I had
heard before that set me free. He said, *Do you feel that?*

I answered, "Yes."

And what happened? He asked.

"Nothing," I responded.

That's right: No matter how it made me feel in that moment, depression did not define me. It did not have power over anything in my

life. It was just a feeling. Nothing less. Nothing more. That is, unless I believed that feeling had power.

But God's gentle voice reminded me, *Don't feel bad for feeling it. Just feel it. Don't fight it. Feel it fully first.* Then He said, *Now that you've felt it, ignore it. It can do no more harm. It will pass like a cloud on a windy day.*

This liberated me. The more I ignored it, the less time it lasted and the less often it came.

And I was reminded that this same wave of emotion was experienced by Jesus. The gospel of Mark gives us an inside look at how He processed it: "Then they went to a place called Gethsemane; and Jesus said to His disciples, 'Sit down here until I have prayed.' He took Peter and James and John with Him, and He began to be deeply distressed and troubled" (Mark 14:32–33 AMP).

Notice the emotions that Jesus experienced as He was getting ready to offer Himself on the cross for you and me: distress and trouble.

We know that Jesus never sinned. In fact, Scripture says, "For we do not have a high priest who is unable to sympathize with our weaknesses, but one who in every respect has been tempted as we are, yet without sin" (Hebrews 4:15 ESV).

You see? Emotions are not sinful. We all have them. But we must learn to not let them have us.

Jesus felt what you feel. He experienced the emotions you are experiencing in your life right now. And He is touched by them. You can go to Him anytime in prayer and receive the mercy, the grace, the help you are looking for in your time of need.

Let's pick up the story at Gethsemane, where Jesus was with Peter, James and John. He said to them:

> My soul is exceeding sorrowful unto death: tarry ye here, and watch. And he went forward a little, and fell on the ground, and prayed that, if it were possible, the hour might pass from him. And he said, Abba, Father, all things are possible unto thee; take away this cup from me: nevertheless not what I will, but what thou wilt.
>
> Mark 14:34–36 KJV

145

While His soul was depressed and exceedingly sorrowful, what did Jesus do?

"He went forward a little."

This is a really powerful way to deal with emotions such as depression. Just move forward a little. The Bible does not say Jesus ran a marathon. He did not even run a fifty-yard dash. He just went forward a little. Sometimes the secret to freedom and healing is simply taking the next small step. Pray for a moment. Send a quick text message of encouragement to someone. Or read a short psalm out loud.

You do not have to fly to the moon. And, by the same token, you do not have to spend hours, weeks or months paralyzed and unable to take action. Just move forward a little.

At Gethsemane, what happened next?

Jesus "fell on the ground."

There is something very powerful about hitting your knees before God. It is not done to earn approval or prove our holiness or act religious. There is a sweet humility in kneeling before the Creator of the universe. It's an act of worship acknowledging our heavenly Father and our need for His strength.

After Jesus fell on the ground, He prayed.

But it was not the kind of prayer we would have expected from the mighty Son of God. He prayed that if it were possible, this cup of suffering and sacrifice would pass and He wouldn't have to drink it. Sometimes prayer is simply a cry to God, saying that we do not want to do what we know we need to do.

And then those beautiful words of Jesus . . . His surrender . . . "Nevertheless not what I will, but Thy will be done."

The act of surrendering to God, abandoning our plans and embracing His, is a powerful way to lift yourself out of the depths of despair and break the cold, dark pain of depression.

I share this story to help you understand the humanity of Jesus. So often, we focus on His divine nature. We forget that He had real feelings, like ours. He felt real emotions, as we do. If you think you are being strong or spiritual by trying to suppress your emotions, you are not. You are making it harder on yourself. Emotions were not meant to be suppressed. They were meant to be expressed. Jesus was fully man and fully God. And in his humanity, he experienced everything you and I have ever felt.

This simple series of steps that Jesus demonstrated in the Garden of Gethsemane has worked for me many times when I have felt down, discouraged or depressed.

⬦ *I've moved forward just a little.* And believe me, sometimes it has been *very* little.

⬦ *I've fallen to my knees.* Not because I am holy but because something happens in your soul when your knees touch the ground.

⬦ *I've prayed.* You do not have to be a prayer warrior. Sometimes the shortest prayer will do. The great apostle Peter once prayed with the simple words "Lord, save me!" (Matthew 14:30). Short prayers are often long enough.

⬦ *I've surrendered.* This sounds harder than it is. So do not be nervous about it. Surrender is just a moment of saying something like what Jesus said, whether you feel it or not: "Father, . . . yet not my will but Thine be done!" (Luke 22:42 Weymouth).

We have to face our life and emotions with honest transparency. This is the first secret to having emotional intelligence. It is being self-aware—knowing that emotions are powerful and constantly changing. And we have to stop pretending that they are not a source of struggle sometimes.

But you do not have to go through the struggle alone. In fact, these moments often call for supernatural strength. Let me share a very powerful passage of Scripture, at the very moment after Jesus' surrender: "Then an angel from heaven appeared and strengthened him" (Luke 22:43 TLB).

Notice when the angel appeared and what he did. When you move forward a little and offer a simple surrender of your will to God's, heaven rains down angel power on you.

Who is ready to feel the strength of an angel? The strength of God?

Moving Forward

Let's "move forward a little" right now.

Have you ever woken up and just did not want to get out of bed? ("Only every day," you might say!) Or have you ever felt anxious or unhappy for no apparent reason?

Well, you are not alone. So have the approximately 350 million people[1] around the globe who suffer from depression, almost eighteen[2] million of them in the United States.

It is a virtual pandemic—the leading cause of disability worldwide[3] and a major contributor to the overall global cost of disease. In America, the economic burden of medical care for people suffering from depression is estimated to be $210 billion per year.[4]

There are many forms of depression—from major depressive disorder to postpartum depression to seasonal depression and even psychotic and bipolar depression. It is enough to fill thousands of medical books with its complexities and challenges.

I want to encourage you *not* to adopt the narrative that you will always suffer from this condition. Do not let yourself be confined or defined by it. Give yourself some grace. So often depression is just a normal reaction to life's stressors—the loss of a loved one, a financial setback, losing a job, going through a family crisis, facing a physical illness.

But sometimes when it hits, it can hit like a hurricane, instantly debilitating and disabling you physically and emotionally.

- You feel distant from God.
- You feel helpless and hopeless, as though you are in an inescapable pit.
- Your energy is depleted.

- ◈ You find it difficult to make decisions.
- ◈ You find yourself overeating or not eating much at all.
- ◈ You are doubting, complaining and worrying all the time.
- ◈ You find yourself oversleeping or unable to sleep at all.
- ◈ You become touchy, fretful or resentful over seemingly minor things.
- ◈ You may even have had thoughts of death or suicide.
- ◈ Instead of light, you feel cast into darkness. Instead of feeling God's strength, you feel powerless.

In this depressed state of mind, you feel burdened and overwhelmed. The crown of God's love is there, but it definitely feels like someone stole it. King David was sure familiar with these feelings: "My guilt has overwhelmed me like a burden too heavy to bear" (Psalm 38:4 NIV).

Remember that in Romans 8:1, Paul shows us that the secret to being free from guilt is not beating ourselves up with condemnation but rather embracing our new identity in Christ: "There is therefore now no condemnation to them which are in Christ Jesus" (KJV).

He goes on to say, "It is God who justifies. Who is he who condemns? It is Christ who died, and furthermore is also risen, who is even at the right hand of God, who also makes intercession for us" (Romans 8:33–34 NKJV).

In your time of need, Jesus stands with you and for you so you can make it to the other side of this emotional storm.

The apostle Paul also gives us the secret to hanging in there when we feel down: "For I am persuaded that neither death nor life, nor angels nor principalities nor powers, nor things present nor things to come, nor height nor depth, nor any other created thing, shall be able to separate us from the love of God which is in Christ Jesus our Lord" (Romans 8:38–39 NKJV).

You see, even the darkest, most demonic forces of depression and anxiety, fear and guilt do not stand a chance when you become convinced that nothing can separate you from God's love. Nothing!

Because that is what depression really is in its simplest form: the feeling of being separated from love. The feeling that there is a gap between how you feel and how you wish you felt.

So what closes that gap? Being convinced that you are loved by God. When sadness and discouragement hit you, God has a remedy: Let His love sweep you away.

Sometimes we forget that God knows what we are going through. He cares deeply about us. He will never be angry with us. He is not shocked that you have the same emotions He has felt.

Sometimes we punish ourselves for feeling bad. And we feel like God could not care less about our little (or big) emotions. There are way more important things for Him to be thinking about, we tell ourselves.

But God is God. He is big enough to take care of all of us. To speak to all of us. To hold hands with all of us. To pull us all up when we are sinking.

I love the way Isaiah describes God's feelings and intentions toward us: "He won't brush aside the bruised and the hurt and he won't disregard the small and insignificant, but he will steadily and firmly set things right" (Isaiah 42:3 MSG).

> He is "near to the brokenhearted and saves the crushed in spirit."

How precious a Savior is our God! He is touched by our feelings. He will not brush us aside. He is "near to the brokenhearted and saves the crushed in spirit" (Psalm 34:18 ESV).

We must know this in our hearts and remind ourselves of it again and again.

Have you ever wondered what causes unhappiness and depression?

Physical, sexual or emotional abuse can certainly make us vulnerable to it. So can a disappointment, loss or serious illness. Genetics (i.e., a family history of depression) can also increase the risk of it. And substance abuse is a huge factor, since nearly 30 percent of people addicted to alcohol or drugs also experience severe depression.[5]

But no matter what the source or cause, millions who suffer from depression seek to escape it. Why? Think back to Pascal, who observed that happiness is the motive behind our every action. Fortunately for us, happiness is not only God's idea, it is also part of God's nature. It flows from Him to us. His Word makes us happy. And His Gospel is the good news of His forgiveness, which begins the process of setting our hearts free.

We know inside that we are supposed to be happy. This mysterious awareness deep within us drives us to feel good, because we know it is what truly satisfies. That is how God created us.

In fact, if you think about it, everything we do in life boils down to two words: pain and pleasure. We are either trying to alleviate pain or obtain some sort of pleasure.

And people relieve their pain in many ways: positively (by praying, exercising and socializing) and negatively (by seeking comfort in substances or people's approval). In fact, all addiction is driven by the ultimate addiction—to happiness. This need for happiness is hardwired into our brains. It is what causes us to scratch that itch.

So we have only one of two motives for every good or bad thing we do: We want to feel pleasure, or we want to alleviate pain. And where can we find the source of all pain?

Look no further than Genesis 2:9 and the Garden of Eden: "And out of the ground the LORD God made to spring up every tree that is pleasant to the sight and good for food. The tree of life was in the midst of the garden, and the tree of the knowledge of good and evil" (ESV).

Notice that God gave Adam and Eve *every* tree pleasing to the eye and good for food. Pleasure was God's idea. Had the first man and first woman continued to eat only from the trees that were pleasing, they would have stayed satisfied.

But when Adam and Eve ate from the one tree that causes pain— the one that gave them the knowledge of good and evil—they became prisoners of pain, unleashing on humankind every form of sorrow, sickness, poverty and negative emotion, including envy, hatred, depression, fear, sadness and shame.

Thus began a downward spiral for humanity. We stopped believing God and started blaming Him and one another. We stopped eating from the trees of pleasure and instead ate from the tree of pain. Condemnation set in, which cascaded into feelings of shame, fear and guilt.

Adam and Eve's fall separated them from God and moved them to make emotionally ruled decisions, rooted in the futile effort to reobtain pleasure and alleviate pain. And independence from God produces profound unhappiness.

But here is the miracle that will set you free: Jesus came to reverse the curse.

Just as eating from the "sin" tree separated humankind from God and unleashed the curse of unhappiness and pain in the world, eating from the Tree of Life reverses the curse and reunites us with God. By going to the cross, Jesus became the Tree of Life for all of us. He took our pain and sorrow upon Himself.

Jesus came to reverse the curse.

When we eat from the Tree of Life, healing begins to take place from within.

This is explained so beautifully in Revelation 22:1–2: "And he shewed me a pure river of water of life, clear as crystal, proceeding out of the throne of God and of the Lamb. . . . And on either side of the river, was there the tree of life . . . and the leaves of the tree were for the healing of the nations" (KJV).

So the route to healing is clear. Eat from the Tree of Life, and you will be healed and satisfied.

Christ has redeemed you from the curse of the law, the curse of unhappiness and pain. The Old Covenant laws point out where we fail and fall short of God's will, and the curse is the consequence of falling short. But no one can obey the law perfectly and escape the consequences of the Fall of humankind. This is the root of all unhappiness. It is the root of condemnation and guilt in our lives.

So God offered us a sacrifice to pay for our sin and our guilt. Jesus became our sacrifice. By doing so, He not only saved us but also freed us from the very root of our unhappiness—our guilt. The removal of our sin and guilt closed the gap that separates us from the presence of God. Now we have bold access to heaven, the right to go to God about anything.

The sickness of our souls came from being separated from the source of true happiness—love. And God is love. This realization frees us from the demonic force of oppressive and depressive emotions.

Love Himself has invited you to His table—to dine with Him, as Jesus said in Revelation 3:20. Believe and receive this glorious invitation!

Because of God's grace, we are no longer emotionally ruled people. We are rescued and ruled by love.

This Knowledge Is Power

Knowing about God's love and sacrifice deals a powerful death blow to the allure of depression and the external pressure that gets inside our souls and weighs us down.

God's presence and love must permeate our thoughts and drown out the negative chatter of inferiority. God's love is the power source of all freedom.

Remember that a sense of powerlessness is the false belief that we are unable to solve our problems, the feeling that we cannot change our circumstances, which in turn results in self-condemnation, hopelessness and depression.

What feeds this sense of powerlessness in life? Our thoughts. So if you want to stop the consequences of a bad temper and heal the sadness and anger within, you have to first change your thoughts.

All our negative self-talk (*Life's a drag. What's the use? I'll never be happy. Things will never change*) weighs us down and weakens us. We are immobilized by the same old recordings running in our heads, ideas that conspire to sink us and kill our joy.

These thoughts march on day after day. According to one study conducted at the University of Maryland School of Medicine, 80 percent of our thoughts are negative, and 95 percent of them are repetitive.[6]

This reveals that the quality of our existence rests on our internal thoughts, which affect our mental and physical health, work and personal relationships. Formed positively, thoughts can give us supernatural strength; formed negatively, they can cut us to the bone.

One trap that keeps us stuck in pain and sorrow is our bad memories. We relive all the hurt and pain we have suffered—the things that were done to us and the mistakes we have made. These memories haunt us. They are on a continuous loop.

In fact, many of us repeatedly rehearse the sad events of our lives and beat ourselves up for what we did wrong. This leaves us imprisoned in our minds. We are like a broken record—stuck, repeating the same sound track again and again.

But remember Romans 14:22: "Happy is the one who does not condemn himself." Think about that.

Since there is no condemnation for those who are in Christ, the more we identify with our new reality—who we are in Christ—the happier we become.

> **The more we identify with who we are in Christ, the happier we become.**

And even when you find yourself being dragged back into your memory closet, realize that God's mercy is "new every morning" (Lamentations 3:23) and that God will finish what He started in your life (see Philippians 1:6).

Bad memories create a pathway to pain; good memories create a pathway to pleasure. We all have both kinds. And we all must choose which ones to focus on. The choice is yours. And that choice empowers you. That is why there is so much in the Bible about remembering what God has done. As it says in Psalm 103:2, "Forget none of His benefits" (NASB 1995).

We must also keep in mind that God treats His people as forgiven. He never brings up our past failure or mistakes: "Their sins and their iniquities will I remember no more" (Hebrews 8:12 KJV).

On top of that, He made us righteous in Christ, and He sees us as He sees Jesus—perfectly holy (see Ephesians 4:24). He even puts us into places of influence and makes us guardians of His galaxy. Believe that, and happiness will surge through your soul.

I am reminded of the legendary nineteenth-century preacher Charles Spurgeon, who often liked to quote Romans 4:8: "Blessed and happy and favored is the man whose sin the Lord will not take into account nor charge against him" (AMP).

So if you are feeling down or depressed, know this: The supreme happiness in life is the assurance that we are forgiven and loved. This reality leads to joy. And nothing else will satisfy us completely except this love connection to God. As the psalmist wrote, "O taste and see that the Lord is good. How happy is the man who trusts in Him!" (Psalm 34:8 NLV).

Trust is simply believing God, no matter what you are going through. It means trusting God's faithfulness to *keep* His promises rather than satisfying our desire to *earn* His promises.

Secrets to Healing Depression

Below are ten essential steps to help you get out from under depression's shadow.

1. Watch over your heart.

Your heart is the "garden center" of your life. Proverbs 4:23 tells us that out of that garden "spring the issues of life" (NKJV). Sure, you are not always in control of your circumstances, but you do have control over your heart—what you choose to plant in it, what you choose to say and believe. In other words, as we plant the seeds of God's promises in our hearts, the fruits of peace and joy will grow in other aspects of our lives. Conversely, if you allow the seeds of fear and negativity to get planted in your heart, they will produce a harvest of depression. But trust me: Depression cannot grow in you and consume you if you are flooding your soul with God's promises. "Let not your heart be troubled" (John 14:1 KJV). How? By believing in Him. And believing in what He said. If you do that, depression will lose its grip.

2. Speak TO your emotion rather than ABOUT it.

So often we feel it is therapeutic to talk about what is bothering us. And in the right setting, there is a time and place for that. But the real key to mastering your emotions is realizing that they are like Siri: You can activate or deactivate them by voice command. Your words have power. So when you feel depressed or anxious, start saying out loud the words that are the opposite of those emotions. This is a one-way conversation you must have with depression and the things weighing down your heart. As Jesus said in Mark 11:23, "Whosoever shall say unto this mountain, Be thou removed, and be thou cast into the sea; and shall not doubt in his heart, . . . he shall have whatsoever he saith" (KJV). Boom!

3. Receive God's gifts.

In John 16:24, Jesus said, "Ask and you will receive, so that your joy may be made full." This passage gives us the key to becoming free from depression: Receive what you ask for, and joy will come. How do you receive? Believe you have whatever you ask for, whether you feel it or not. *Act as if.* Faith says, *I got it. It might not look like it or feel like it, but I got it.*

4. Thank and praise God.

Thank God for the blessings in your life—if you just stop and write down some of the things you are grateful for, and say them out loud, your emotional condition will immediately improve. Your emotions do not have a choice. They respond to your choice and your voice. The Word of God says that praise stills the avenger (see Psalm 8:2). It breaks the back of depression and its ugly cousins anxiety and negativity.

In fact, you cannot stay depressed for very long if you start praising God. But so often we are focused on what we do not have, which weighs down our hearts and makes us feel bad about our lives.

In a University of California study about successful people's secret to happiness, it was discovered that a common trait was that they appreciate what they have. Taking time to focus on what they were grateful for was not merely the right thing to do; it also improved their moods, energy and physical well-being because it reduced the stress hormone cortisol by 23 percent.[7]

This reminds me of Romans 1:21: "For although they knew God, they neither glorified him as God nor gave thanks to him, but their thinking became futile and their foolish hearts were darkened" (NIV). We do not want a dark heart—or futile thoughts, which can lead to mental disorders.

So where to start? Thank Him for the gift of *life* and the gift of *eternal* life. Thank Him for the people in your life. Thank Him for His daily provision for your life. Thank Him for another chance to get your attitude going in the right direction. Life is a gift. People are gifts. Our jobs, businesses, opportunities are gifts. Express that reality by thanking God for them. You will not be able to stay depressed if you keep thanking Him.

5. Stop condemning yourself.

Depression corrodes our confidence and brings with it a sense of shame and incessant self-blame. We get caught in a loop of beating ourselves up and blaming ourselves for who we are or what we have done. But condemnation is a mindset that robs you of joy and peace. Do not condemn yourself, because God does not condemn you. One of the best ways to tackle self-blame is to forgive yourself. We are human. We make mistakes. How do you forgive yourself? It is a decision to say aloud to yourself, "I forgive myself, because God has already forgiven me." Remember, "There is *now no* condemnation for those who are in Christ Jesus" (Romans 8:1 NIV, emphasis added). Get your "now no" praise on!

6. Understand that God is still working on you.

Philippians 1:6 tells us: "He who began a good work in you will bring it to completion at the day of Jesus Christ" (ESV). So we need to lighten up on ourselves. He began a good work in you; He will finish it. Trust God that you are a work in progress. You are not standing still. This image of God working in us is woven throughout Scripture: "And now you are living stones that are being used to build a spiritual house" (1 Peter 2:5 CEV). Think of the Lord as having a chisel in his hand, cutting away the pieces that do not belong, fashioning us according to His plan. In Ephesians 2:10, we are described as God's workmanship, his masterpiece. And so it is. And so you are.

7. Tap into the power of believing.

Studies demonstrate that belief in God is linked to a reduction in symptoms of depression, including the deep sense of hopelessness that is the trademark of this condition. The power of believing can move mountains, including emotional ones. Speak to that mountain and believe it will move. Following is the most simple and profound way I have ever read it in Scripture: "May the God of hope fill you with all joy and peace in believing" (Romans 15:13 AMP). If you are lacking joy and peace, check what you are believing. Are you believing the bad reports from the media and world around you? Or are you believing the good report of God's promises?

Ready for the nail in the coffin of depression? Let this one seal the deal: "Even though you do not see him now, you believe in him and are filled with an inexpressible and glorious joy" (1 Peter 1:8 NIV). Believe these promises, regardless of what you feel, and depression will begin to die.

8. Reject shame.

So often I have seen people feel ashamed about struggling. Remember, you are *not* your struggle. You may struggle, but it is not who you are. You are a son or daughter of God. You are a part of His royal family.

You have real emotions. It is what makes you, you. Do not ever let the enemy shame you for feeling depressed or anxious. It is not your fault. And it is not abnormal. Do not let anyone shame you. Do not let yourself shame you. Sometimes when you are battling emotions, it drains you. You are not as productive as you usually are, so you judge yourself as weak or a failure. Those are lies. Reject them. Give yourself grace. Remind yourself that Jesus took your shame on the cross. No matter what you feel or what you have done, God is not ashamed of you. He is proud of you. You bring Him joy. And we are all dealing with something. If you feel darkness, know that God is with you, even in the valley.

9. Surround yourself with positive people.

The people we associate with rub off on us, for better or worse. I call this the power of association. That is why we need to be picky about our friends. Because being around happy people can help alleviate depression. Happiness and positive thinking are contagious. So align yourself with friends, family and colleagues who create an atmosphere of faith and expectation with their attitude and words. As Paul said in 1 Corinthians 15:33, "Bad company corrupts good morals" (AMP). The flip side is true, too: Good company corrupts bad morals. And we should leverage that knowledge fully in our lives. Choose the good. Choose to spend time with positive people full of faith—people who reject negativity and pessimism—and who will call you out when your faith starts waning. And keep those people in your life.

10. Be aware that you are not helpless or powerless.

You are not helpless or powerless: these twin lies keep us enslaved to depression. And God has provided just what you need to evict these lies from the belief center of your soul: "For He Himself has said, I will not in any way fail you nor give you up nor leave you without support. . . . [I will] not in any degree leave you helpless nor forsake nor let [you] down" (Hebrews 13:5 AMPC). So we must reinforce this truth in our souls. God is holding us. He is helping us. He is present with us.

This allows us to come into our power: "So we take comfort and are encouraged and confidently and boldly say, The Lord is my Helper; I will not be seized with alarm. . . . What can man do to me?" (Hebrews 13:6 AMPC). Wow!

God is a "very present help" in your time of need (Psalm 46:1 KJV). He will never let you go.

The Holy Spirit is your helper. He has not left you alone, and He never will.

And now you have the power to pray and receive the answer—the joy of God's presence.

DECIDE AND DECLARE

- ◈ I am deeply loved by God and no longer separated from Him.
- ◈ I will not be controlled by depression anymore.
- ◈ I am filled with faith and optimism.
- ◈ I reject negativity and pessimism.
- ◈ I am neither helpless nor hopeless, because I have the Holy Spirit living in me.

NOW PRAY THIS WITH ME

Today, I embrace Your love, God. Thank You for Your presence, Your forgiveness and Your approval, which empower me to stop condemning myself for my shortcomings. With Your love, I have power over my emotions.

Knowing all this, I command every vestige and residue of depression to leave my life. I command it to be removed and cast into the sea, in Jesus' name! Amen.

11

Shame Off You!

Shame is a soul-eating emotion.
Carl Jung

The enemy of our soul is shame. It swallows men whole.
Gregory Dickow

I don't know about you, but I sure don't want my soul eaten. Nor do I want my "whole" eaten.

But that is how powerful shame is. It is a crushing force that I am on a mission to destroy. And I want to help you imagine just how powerful you will be when we rip shame's throat out.

I am using strong language regarding this demonic force because it is perhaps the number one thing standing in the way of your greatness and emotional freedom.

Shame corrodes the part of us that believes we were created for greatness. It convinces us that we are flawed and unworthy of love and belonging, unworthy of receiving what we need from God.

Shame is always rooted in the erroneous thought that *I'm not enough, I can never be enough, and God is not going to give me enough.*

161

It finds its roots in rejection and in the ignorance of our redeemed innocence and grace-purchased identity that was procured for us when Jesus took our shame on the cross.

> Shame is what stands between us and an answered prayer.

Shame is what stands between us and an answered prayer.

Jesus tells a story about a man who had no food. So the man goes to his friend late at night and asks to borrow three loaves of bread. The friend responds, "Don't bother me! The door is already locked, and my children and I have gone to bed. I can't get up to give you anything" (Luke 11:7 CSB).

Jesus goes on to say: "I tell you this—though he won't do it for friendship's sake, if you keep knocking long enough, he will get up and give you whatever you need because of your *shameless* persistence" (Luke 11:8 NLT, emphasis added).

This story will help us see why the enemy of our souls wants to keep us in shame.

The "friend" of this man had four layers of excuses why he would not help.

1. *Don't bother me.* He did not want to be inconvenienced.
2. *The door is locked.* Are *you* facing a door that will not open?
3. *We are already in bed. It's too late.* Does it feel like it is too late for *your* life to get better?
4. *I "can't" get up and give you anything.* Are *you* up against a "can't" in your life?

Yet there was one reason this man got everything he needed: He had no shame.

Jesus said it was the man's "shameless persistence" that caused him to receive everything he needed. One translation (CEV) says he was "not ashamed to keep on asking."

No wonder the enemy of our souls wants us living in shame. The devil knows that when we are shameless before God, we will keep asking Him for whatever we need and that our prayers will ultimately be answered.

But because of shame, people give up too soon.

How does shame rob us of answered prayers? Because doubt, as the late psychoanalyst Erik Erikson said, is "the brother of shame."[1]

So when we feel a sense of shame, it brings doubt with it. We doubt our lives could dramatically improve. We doubt God will meet our needs. We doubt we are worthy of great love. We doubt our prayers will be answered. We doubt our destiny. We doubt ourselves—all because of shame. Shame makes us give up when faced with resistance or opposition.

Fans of survival films might remember one of my favorite movies, *The Edge*. In it, a private plane carrying billionaire Charles Morse (Anthony Hopkins) crashes in the Alaskan wilderness. There are two survivors with him, a photographer, Robert (Alec Baldwin), and his assistant, Stephen. Charles, always reading and learning, tries to give hope to his companions, devising a plan to help them reach civilization.

The biggest obstacle, however, might not be the elements or even the man-eating bear stalking them. Instead, it is a deeper enemy lurking within the human soul.

At one point, the following conversation ensues:

Charles: You know, I once read an interesting book which said that most people lost in the wilds, they die of shame.
Stephen: What?
Charles: Yeah, see, they die of shame. "What did I do wrong? How could I have gotten myself into this?" And so they sit there and they die. Because they didn't do the one thing which would save their lives. Thinking.[2]

Charles knows that the shame people feel has the potential to defeat them. It paralyzes them and robs them of solution-centered thinking. It can thwart the human survival mechanism that God hardwired into our brains. And it can push us to wither away in the "wilderness" because we feel we deserve it.

Your personal wilderness could be anything—a feeling of having just barely enough; a sense that you will never be able to overcome, never be able to break through.

The scene from *The Edge* really speaks to me because it is a reminder that, in our own journeys, so often we are just trying to get "home" to where we belong. But somehow we feel like life is getting even with us. Shame's lie is that we somehow deserve to suffer and die in the wilderness. Shame pushes us to wither away in mediocrity and unfulfilled potential.

Unlike guilt, which is the feeling that we did something wrong, shame is the feeling of *being* something wrong. It is a private feeling within your soul that you are defective as a person, irreparably damaged.

Everyone wants to find home—that safe place inside where we are free to be ourselves, to love ourselves, to enjoy our existence and to embrace life, despite its complexities and challenges, without judgment or blame. But then there is the obstacle of shame, that painful sense that there is a dark secret in your soul—some embarrassing or disgusting or weak aspect about you that is about to get exposed.

So many people are dying in the wilderness, so to speak, because of shame.

Shame hijacks your inner voice of confidence, saying, *The reason you are living below your potential rather than assuming your true identity and destiny is because you are being punished. You don't deserve to live better. You deserve to be defeated, because there's something wrong with you.*

I felt that way as a teenager and even for several years after becoming a Christian. I easily embraced self-accusation and condemnation. It felt familiar, accurate and right. Under this bondage of shame, the lies in my head disguised themselves as truth.

People who are ashamed of themselves become convinced that they are innately defective. Yes, we are human and flawed, but we are *not* condemned as irreparably broken.

Whether we are aware of our shame or not, it feeds soul thieves such as depression, fear and anger. These toxic emotions reinforce the negative view of ourselves that in turn leads to self-defeating behaviors and conditions: addiction, obsession, outbursts of anger, violence, sexual assault, social anxiety—you name it. Hmm. That pretty much sums up everything we are dealing with in the world today.

It is a vicious cycle. The more shame we feel, the more driven we are to behaviors that make us feel even more shameful. And down we go. As Paul wrote in Romans 7:19, "For I do not do the good I want, but the evil I do not want is what I keep on doing" (ESV).

When you are imprisoned by shame, you feel insignificant, almost invisible. Shame doesn't actually make you insignificant or inferior, it just makes you *feel* like you are.

SHAME'S UGLY CHECKLIST:

- ◈ you feel you do not belong
- ◈ you feel there is something wrong with you
- ◈ you feel you are irreparably broken
- ◈ you feel you deserve the bad because you are bad

You see, in the Garden of Eden, the serpent got Eve thinking that she was "less than" God, even though God made her in His own image. It was only then that she felt "less than." And then she made a choice that was "less than." And then she *became* "less than." And lived "less than."

The serpent said, "God knows that the day you eat from [that tree], your eyes will be opened, and you will be like God" (Genesis 3:5 EHV).

The deception of that statement was that Eve was *already like God*, made in His image from the beginning of creation (see Genesis 1:27). The enemy of Eve's soul got her feeling shame ("less than"), and then she made a decision from this inferior frame of mind—this errone-ous mindset.

As a result, Adam and Eve both felt like there was something wrong with them and attempted to compensate for what they thought was missing. "When the woman saw that the tree was good for food, and that it was a delight to the eyes, and that the tree was desirable to make one wise, she took some of its fruit and ate; and she also gave some to her husband with her, and he ate" (Genesis 3:6).

Adam and Eve's shame-driven belief that they were incomplete led them to do something they thought would complete them—but in fact it destroyed them.

Once shame entered the picture, they lost their souls. Instead of lifting their heads high with a positive sense of self-worth, they put their heads down in shame.

It is important to realize that Eve did not sin because there was something wrong with her, but rather because she *thought* there was something wrong with her. Her behavior mirrored what she believed about herself, even though her belief was false.

> Eve did not sin because there was something wrong with her, but rather because she *thought* there was something wrong with her.

Likewise, the reason you and I sin and make hurtful decisions is not because we are evil. It is because we are trying to heal something that is broken inside us. We are trying to fix the shame, the force that is robbing us of our true value and worth—our crowns (see chapter 9).

Remember, condemnation robs you of confidence before God, so you cannot receive His blessing or gifts, because you doubt you are worthy to receive them. Genesis 3:17–19 says:

Cursed is the ground because of you; in pain you shall eat of it all the days of your life; thorns and thistles it shall bring forth for you; and you shall eat the plants of the field. By the sweat of your face you shall eat bread, till you return to the ground, for out of it you were taken; for you are dust, and to dust you shall return. (ESV)

Notice the phrase "till you return to the ground." I would add: "And to the ground you will look."

You see, shame "grounds" us. It makes us look down. Rather than soaring like an eagle, living the free and full life that we were originally created for, we live low lives, adhering to self-imposed limitations.

Which came first, the chicken or the . . . eagle?

Perhaps you have heard the fable of the farmer who found an eagle's egg one day and, thinking it was one of his chicken's eggs, placed it in a nest in his chicken coop. The egg hatched with those of the chickens, and the baby eagle grew up thinking he was a chicken. The eagle did what the chickens did. It scratched the dirt for seeds and worms. It did not fly more than a few feet off the ground, because this is what the chickens did.

One day the bird saw an eagle flying gracefully and majestically high above him. He asked an older chicken friend, "What is that beautiful bird? I want to fly like him one day."

The chicken said, "Don't be silly. That's an eagle. He's the most glorious bird. But you will never fly like him. That's not who you are. You're just a chicken. Don't even think about it."

So the eagle never gave it a second thought. And he lived and died as a chicken.

Shame is that chicken telling you that you will never fly like an eagle. Shame silences your dreams, clips your wings and keeps you believing you are "less than."

What else does shame do?

- Shame robs you of the confidence you need to be great.
- Shame makes you self-conscious (the feeling that you are observed but not approved).

♦ Shame makes you sin-conscious (always aware of your mistakes).

♦ Shame stops you from dreaming of a better life.

♦ Shame activates the stress response, releasing negative hormones such as cortisol, which breaks down the immune system.

♦ Shame makes you accept life the way it is (saying, "You don't deserve anything better").

♦ Shame makes you stop looking up in prayer and expectation.

In short, shame reduces you and makes you small, destroying your self-worth and, with it, your potential. So instead of being bold, you become passive. You look down and stay down.

How do we break out of this grounded condition?

Breaking out of Shame

The devil and man-made religion want to trap us in in the belief that we are "falling short." This keeps us defeated and limited, hemmed in by our human nature rather than liberated through our God-given divine nature. Second Peter 1:4 says, "He has given to us exceedingly great and precious promises, so that through these things you might become partakers of the divine nature and escape the corruption that is in the world through lust" (MEV).

So how do we break this vicious cycle of shame, which corrupts our world?

It starts with a shift in our focus. Shame causes us to judge ourselves, examine our flaws, see ourselves as defective. This is actually "me-centered," not "Jesus-centered." In Hebrews 12:2 (NKJV), Paul calls us to look to Jesus—"the author and finisher of our faith"—rather than looking within.

After all, looking within all the time can depress us. We seem to take life's magnifying glass and magnify what we do not like about ourselves and others rather than putting the magnifying glass on Jesus. By magnifying Him, we are not making Him bigger. He is already as big as big can be. We are just making Him look bigger *in our eyes.*

It may seem humble to magnify our flaws, but in actuality it is truly humble to magnify what God has done for us—loved us, forgiven us and made us a part of His royal family. This starts with developing a righteousness-consciousness rather than a sin-consciousness. Righteousness means to be in right standing with God, without guilt, shame, inferiority or fear. Sin-consciousness gets us to turn the magnifying glass on our sins and shortcomings.

Believing that we are redeemed from shame positions us to confidently possess God's promises for our lives. It lets us behave as if we are free from the pain of the past.

The awareness of our flaws can be crippling, but God has provided a solution.

1. Fix your eyes on his rights rather than your wrongs.

Be Christ-absorbed, and you will no longer be self-absorbed.

2. Understand the beautiful gift of righteousness.

Paul wrote in 2 Corinthians 5:21, "For our sake he made him to be sin who knew no sin, so that in him we might become the righteousness of God" (ESV). This is the greatest exchange in human history. Jesus took our sinfulness on the cross and imparted to us His righteousness, which means we are right in God's eyes, not wrong. As a new creation in Christ, you are His righteousness. This understanding is what set me free from the constant condemnation and shame that my old life without God had wired into my brain.

3. Replace sin-consciousness with righteousness-consciousness.

Sin-consciousness is to be ever aware of your sins, flaws and mistakes. Righteousness-consciousness is to be ever aware of your position in Christ. This state of being seated with Christ, being eternally in right standing with God, is nothing short of a miracle. As it penetrates your mind, you are rewiring your brain to embrace your acceptance and approval from God. That is how shame loses its power over you.

4. Focus on right-being rather than right-doing.

When you understand that righteousness is "right-being," your "doing," or your behavior, begins to mirror the way you see yourself. A beautiful verse in the Bible says that when you awaken to the reality about who you are and how God sees you, it will change your behavior: "Awake to righteousness, and sin not" (1 Corinthians 15:34 KJV).

5. Stop thinking "BC" (before Christ).

You and I were a total mess without Jesus. But you have been recreated in Christ Jesus, and you are now in Him. There is nothing wrong in Him. Therefore there is nothing wrong in you. You have flaws, as I do. But the core of your being, as a child of God, is good. As this permeates your thinking, you feel a rush of freedom that is not easy to describe in words. But it is emotional freedom as it was meant to be.

6. Put into the past everything you used to think about yourself.

The opinion you have previously formed of yourself is like an old library book—past due. Send it back to where it came from. It is not the real you. The genuine new you is a blood-bought, blood-washed child of God—reigning as a victor in this life (see Revelation 1:5–6).

Notable psychiatrist Carl Jung once said, "The most terrifying thing is to accept oneself completely."[3] But it is not hard to accept yourself when you realize that you no longer have to cover up your defects or distract yourself from them. Your soul is a work of art. And the artist is God, not you. Also, you can accept yourself completely because you are a work in progress. Look at how the Word of God describes you: "For we are God's masterpiece. He has created us anew in Christ Jesus, so we can do the good things he planned for us long ago" (Ephesians 2:10 NLT).

Even here God puts the concept of *being* first. Then doing. We *are*. Then we *do*. Doing the good things God has planned flows from knowing who we are and whose we are.

And the Verdict Is . . . Not Guilty!

Sometimes we confuse shame with guilt, a related but quite different emotion.

When you feel shame, you are telling yourself, *I'm bad.*

When you feel guilty, you are telling yourself, *I've done something bad.* Or, *I've failed to do something I should've done.*

A guilty conscience leaves you feeling terrible, as if you are not living up to God's "standards." I am convinced that multitudes of believers are suffering from the sickness called guilt, which eats them alive. Nothing seems to rob us of our true vitality and purpose—our true joy and rest—more than guilt.

Maybe you are struggling right now with a guilty secret, a lie you told that caused other people pain. Or maybe you feel guilty because you said something in anger that you later regretted. Or there could be a sexual sin in your recent or ancient history or a selfish mistake that destroyed all trust. Or maybe you betrayed a friend who left you out in the cold.

Maybe you cannot pay back a debt or you feel guilty about overeating. Maybe you feel guilty because you cannot finish your to-do list or do not spend enough time at home with your family. On and on. Or maybe you feel guilty merely because you never measure up.

So we accuse ourselves of our inadequacies and pronounce ourselves guilty and condemned. You know the inner voices:

◈ *You never do enough for your kids, parents or friends.*
◈ *You don't get it all done.*
◈ *You blow it when you're making progress.*
◈ *You say things you regret.*

- *You get angry too easily.*
- *You don't have the right clothes.*
- *You eat too much.*
- *You don't exercise enough.*
- *You don't pray enough.*
- *You don't serve enough.*

Sound familiar? We are so weighed down with these accusations that we begin to believe them.

On a whole other level, perhaps you feel the burden of guilt for something that was done *to* you, some form of abuse that left you feeling both ashamed and guilty. Victims of childhood abuse sometimes blame themselves and feel shame and guilt even though the abuse was not their fault. Isn't it the perpetrators who should be feeling our guilt and shame?

Such abuse leaves people feeling like their entire selves are wrong, that they are defective and damaged, that there is no cure for their shame. I would go a step further: All that blended guilt and shame can make people feel like they actually deserve the bad things that have happened in their lives. And that could not be further from the truth.

Ironically, like shame, guilt causes us to continue our destructive behaviors and make the bad decisions that follow from them, fueling even more guilt. Remember Romans 7:19? "For I do not do the good I want, but the evil I do not want is what I keep on doing" (ESV).

Guilt also causes us to make promises to God that we cannot keep. *I'll never do that again. I'll be better next time.* Yet the pattern repeats itself anyway.

Enough! Everyone needs to feel relieved of guilt, absolved of it. And the human heart will do almost anything to banish it. We can either temporarily cover it up with excuses and self-destructive behaviors, or we can experience the depths of God's grace, which will completely liberate us from guilt forever. If you are like me, you are choosing grace and liberty.

I love Job 10:7: "According to Your knowledge I am indeed not guilty." Notice that Job says, "According to Your knowledge"—God's knowledge. As far as He is concerned, we are not guilty.

This is very different from our perception of ourselves. According to us, and even according to the opinions of other people—we are guilty. We are aware of our own sins, mistakes, shortcomings and failures. But according to God's knowledge, we can live a life free from guilt, condemnation and misery. You see, we have to choose which opinion of ourselves we will embrace: our own or God's. "In Him we have redemption through His blood, the forgiveness of our trespasses, according to the riches of His grace" (Ephesians 1:7).

> "In Him we have redemption through His blood, the forgiveness of our trespasses, according to the riches of His grace."

The judgment for your sins has already been paid by Christ. Jesus' taking the punishment settles forever your debt before God. Remember that God says, "There is now no condemnation for those who are in Christ Jesus" (Romans 8:1 NIV).

You *can* live free! It starts in Hebrews 10:22, in this beautiful passage from the New Living Translation: "Let us go right into the presence of God with sincere hearts fully trusting him. For our guilty consciences have been sprinkled with Christ's blood to make us clean, and our bodies have been washed with pure water."

Notice that Paul said, "Our guilty consciences have been sprinkled with Christ's blood to make us clean." He does not say that "our apologies" or "our good efforts" make us clean. I am not saying that we should not do good things. But none of those things cleanses us from a guilty conscience.

There is only one thing that cleanses us from a guilty conscience: the blood of Jesus Christ. He sprinkles us with His blood once and for all.

Time to Peel the Paint off the Wall

Have you ever seen one of those heavy-duty golf-course sprinklers that is so powerful it can knock you off your feet? I am not talking about a fun summertime soft-rainbow sprinkler—the kind you used to jump in and out of as a kid. Those things could barely get you wet!

I am talking about something that has super strength. That is the kind of sprinkler God uses to cleanse us of our sins—the kind that can peel the paint off the wall. The blood of Jesus peels all the sin right off of us.

It peels off all the condemnation, all the guilt, all the shame, all the regret, all the mistakes and all the shortcomings. And all that is left is you, washed by the precious blood of Jesus, God's Lamb, no longer having to live with a guilty conscience.

So whatever you have done, no matter how powerfully bad it is, *it is gone*. It is washed away. You have been cleansed. Jesus' blood cleanses you forever and renders you free from guilt.

This is what it is like to be free from guilt and shame forever.

◈ You will feel a sense of liberating freedom.
◈ You will feel energized, because guilt sucks the life out of you and joy out of life.
◈ You will feel emboldened to dream big and ask big.
◈ You will forgive other people freely because you realize that you are forgiven freely.
◈ You will be a magnet for other people, drawing them toward freedom through your joy.
◈ You will stop beating yourself up.
◈ You will have confidence before God, so that whatever you ask, you will receive from Him.
◈ You will walk in the power of God.

◈ You will become the best version of yourself.
◈ You will be able to handle mistakes, weaknesses and criticisms without crumbling.
◈ You will not be manipulated by other people through guilt, nor will you manipulate them.

In short, you do not have to live with guilt another day of your life. Jesus has destroyed all the evidence against you. Oh, it was there. Make no mistake about it. But your Advocate Defender, Jesus, has erased the evidence with His blood. And now He presents you before the Father, God, and declares you *not guilty*.

So from this day forward, you are going to live a guilt-free life.

But to do that, we must still identify the ways in which the enemy works to undermine us and paint us with guilt and condemnation in the first place. So what can we do when we feel the harsh breath of the devil breathing down our necks, making us feel profoundly flawed, defective and incomplete?

Look at Romans 8:32: "He who did not spare His own Son, but delivered Him over for us all, how will He not also with Him freely give us all things?"

I always wondered why the next verse says, "Who will bring a charge against God's elect?" (NASB 1995). Verse 32 reveals that in Jesus, God gave us all things freely. But *we are* the ones bringing a charge against God's elect. There is something in our heads—this guilt-ridden mentality—that says, *I don't deserve it.*

God responds: *It's free.*

We protest: *Oh, I haven't earned it.*

But it is free!

I haven't done enough to get it.

But Jesus is telling us it is free. You do not have to do anything except receive it.

The thing is, Satan is accusing you. Every time God gives you a promise, Satan gives you an accusation. So God says, "Freely, I give you all things," but you are being accused by the enemy: *Well, you don't deserve it. You can't have it. You haven't done enough. Look at what you have done, and look at how you failed.* And that is why the apostle Paul combats those inner conversations in verses 33–34: "Who will bring charges [accusations] against God's elect? God is the one who justifies; who is the one who condemns? Christ Jesus is He who died, but rather, was raised, who is at the right hand of God, who also intercedes for us." No matter what you have done, no matter how much the devil tries to accuse you and tell you, *You don't deserve it; you're not worthy of God's blessing,* God is showing us how to respond to that guilt. That is why Paul said in verse 31, "What then shall we say to these things?"

We ask, *Who will bring charges against God's elect? God is the one who justifies; who is the one who condemns?* We should add, "Therefore there is now no condemnation at all for those who are in Christ Jesus. . . . Who will separate us from the love of Christ?" (Romans 8:1, 35).

These are the simple truths that will set us free from guilt and condemnation forever.

Let's Change It Today

So just as we laid out the steps to counteract the force of shame in our lives, let's lay out the steps to counteract guilt.

1. Declare yourself not guilty.

If you declare yourself not guilty, it does not mean that you have not previously sinned or done nothing wrong. It does mean that Jesus has washed away all your sin and guilt with His blood. "It was fitting for us to have such a high priest, holy, innocent, undefiled . . . who has no daily need . . . to offer up sacrifices . . . because He did this once for all time when He offered up Himself" (Hebrews 7:26–27).

2. See yourself as God sees you.

Accept the message of Colossians 1:22, which says that through Jesus' blood, He presents you "holy and faultless and irreproachable" in the Father's eyes (AMPC). When God sees you, He sees you as He sees Jesus—just as Isaac saw his son Jacob as if he were Esau (see Genesis 27). And your heavenly Father sees you as if you were Jesus—without guilt.

3. Go with God's knowledge over your own.

God knows better than you do, so give Him the benefit of the doubt. "According to Your knowledge I am indeed not guilty" (Job 10:7). As far as you are concerned, you are guilty. But as far as God is concerned, you are not guilty.

4. When you blow it, do not deny it.

Whenever you make a mistake, feel it. Reveal it to God and let Him heal it. It is incredibly therapeutic to get something off your chest. Take it to God. He already knows. He already forgave you. Just talking to Him about it empowers you to be honest with yourself.

5. It is already done.

Believe that the work of washing away your sins is already done. The last words of Jesus on the cross were "It is finished" (John 19:30). Notice He did not say, "I did My half. Now you do yours." At the moment He breathed His last, the price was paid for your sin and guilt. Hebrews 1:3 says, "When he had cleansed us from our sins, he sat down in the place of honor at the right hand of the majestic God in heaven" (NLT).

6. Stop thinking that you have to feel guilty to be forgiven.

Sometimes we think we owe it to people to feel guilty for everything. Stop thinking that. You do not owe anyone. Do not think that your guilt somehow pays for something. The blood of Jesus paid it all. When we feel like we owe God guilt or we owe it to others to wallow in guilt, we remain trapped.

7. Stop beating yourself up about what you have not done.

We often punish ourselves with self-condemnation. We feel like we will never do enough for God. But that is why Jesus did it all. He paid for our sins and our failures. Our job is to believe it and say it.

The way to silence the accusers, the soul thieves of guilt and shame, is through words. So say out loud what Jesus has done for you. Make the declaration below whenever you feel the slightest shred of guilt or shame. The result? You become the devil's worst nightmare every day of your life.

"The accuser of our brothers and sisters has been thrown down. . . . And they overcame him because of the blood of the Lamb and because of the word of their testimony" (Revelation 12:10–11).

DECIDE AND DECLARE

◈ I am loved, washed and forgiven in Jesus.
◈ I am saved, healed and redeemed in Him.
◈ I am not irreparably damaged. I am God's masterpiece.
◈ I am a king and priest before Him.
◈ I am justified and delivered from the curse of guilt and shame.
◈ I am free!

NOW PRAY THIS WITH ME

Jesus, thank You for loving me, washing me and forgiving me. You not only saved me, but You healed me, redeemed me and made me a king and priest before You. I am so grateful that You delivered me from the curse of guilt and shame. Nothing can separate me from Your love. And nothing can shame or condemn me or make me feel guilty another day of my life unless I let it. No one can bring a charge against me anymore. It is You who has justified me, raised me up and seated me with You. In Your precious name, I pray, Amen.

12

Anger

The Poison Pill

Go ahead and be angry. You do well to be angry—but don't use your anger as fuel for revenge. And don't stay angry. Don't go to bed angry. Don't give the Devil that kind of foothold in your life.

Ephesians 4:26 MSG

A recently divorced woman, traveling in Morocco, stumbled across an antique lamp. As she dusted it off a bit—you guessed it—out popped a genie.

"I will grant you three wishes," the genie told her, "but on one condition. Your ex-husband will get double whatever you ask for."

"Okay," she cheerfully responded. "I wish for a billion dollars."

"It is granted," the genie answered. "But your ex-husband gets two billion dollars."

"Now I wish for a beautiful paradise-like estate on the Mediterranean Sea," the woman gushed, "with an infinity pool, tennis courts and staff serving me night and day."

"Granted! Now, remember," the genie explained, "your ex-husband gets double whatever you ask for. So make your final wish."

The woman thought about it for a moment, recalling how much pain her ex-husband caused her, then said, "Okay, genie, for my last wish, I want you to beat me half to death."

Ouch!

You know there is some element of truth in every joke. That is what makes it funny. But in my thirty years of ministry experience, I have never condoned violence or encouraged anyone to take revenge. I believe God will avenge us, and He will right every wrong. And that belief is probably the greatest contributing factor to what has set me free from the titanic power of anger and rage.

This insidious "demon" of anger is the most lethal thief of the soul.

Give Yourself Permission to Be Angry: God Did

Most of us know all too well the familiar feelings of anger. At times, it will come upon us instantaneously, as a visceral response to a hurt, injustice or threat. And sometimes anger can be a good thing, as an effective way of surviving and protecting ourselves from danger. It is part of our fight-or-flight response, a normal reaction to an event or attack that threatens us.

But often it disguises itself, giving us the false promise of freedom or release. It lures us into believing it will make us feel vindicated and will make things right. But after that momentary satisfaction, anger usually leaves us in pain. And we have all been there.

It is not a sin to feel anger.

The good news is this: It is not a sin to feel anger. And we do not have to run away from God because of it. In fact, God tells us, "Be angry, and yet do not sin" (Ephesians 4:26). So give yourself permission to feel anger. Because that's how the healing process begins.

Hebrews 4:15 says, "We do not have a high priest who cannot sympathize with our weaknesses, but One who has been tempted in all things just as we are, yet without sin." Jesus was tempted in every way:

with lust, with fear, with anger, with depression. He had all the feelings you have, yet He never sinned. But He is familiar with the weapons Satan brings to defeat you. He understands the impulse to quit and give up on His calling and give up on His purpose. But in the end, He mastered His emotions rather than letting them master Him.

Jesus demonstrates for us that we can have emotions without them having us. That is what I want for you. More importantly, that is what God wants for you.

You see, God does not want us to feel bad about the emotions we have. Instead, He wants us to experience emotional *freedom* from shame, freedom from the need to retaliate—freedom from fear, depression, sadness and sorrow.

> You can have emotions without them having you.

So yes, we have been tempted and have sinned. In fact, there are times when we veer out of control, when anger can morph into violence, driven by intense feelings of antagonism, fear, anxiety and hatred. Whether it is the 82 percent[1] of drivers in America who admit to road rage or the approximately 10 percent of American adults who struggle with impulsive angry behavior,[2] anger is all around us.

It is important that we not minimize the effects of anger in our lives, but learn how to process it through the wisdom and power of God.

Without the gentle guidance of the Holy Spirit, anger can lead to arguments, physical fights, emotional and physical abuse, assault and self-harm, even homicide and suicide. So to call uncontrolled anger a powerful emotion is an understatement. It is a nuclear button that we need to gracefully dismantle.

In a state of intense anger, our bodies instantly go into fight-or-flight mode. Our adrenal glands react immediately, flooding our bodies with stress hormones such as adrenaline and cortisol. The brain goes on high alert and directs blood away from the stomach and toward the muscles in preparation for a fight. Our heart rate, blood pressure and respiration spike, while our body temperature rises. And that is not all.

Studies prove that anger is linked to a high risk of heart attack, stroke, migraines, and drug and alcohol addiction. It also contributes to obesity, insomnia and depression. In fact, in the two hours after an angry outburst, the chance of having a heart attack quintuples, and the chance of having a stroke triples.[3]

This is why I believe God tells us, "Do not let the sun go down on your anger" (Ephesians 4:26). So as long as it is still light outside, go ahead and stay mad. You're good!

But seriously, the human mind and body were not designed to carry these emotions for very long. From an emotional standpoint, anger fuels low self-esteem, worry, anxiety and mental fatigue—so-called brain fog. It destroys happiness in the home and leads to low-quality relationships and a high probability of abusing yourself and others. In short, anger is a poison pill. And that is why we have to root out this mammoth soul thief and put it in its place.

A Matter of Perspective

How do we put anger in its place? It is all about a gift I call perspective.

How is perspective a gift? Because with a shift in the way you look at something, you are activating God's gift of peace, which dilutes anger's power.

That is, instead of seeing life as happening *to* you, you can start seeing life as happening *for* you (see pages 84, 141). This one shift in perspective can change your life forever.

It is the "two-by-four" (think lumber) that needs to hit you squarely in the head. The difference between "to" and "for" is everything.

In fact, did you know that in the Chinese alphabet, the symbol for "crisis" is the same as the symbol for "opportunity"? You can embrace the things that happen in your life as a continual crisis or a continual opportunity. A continual crisis mindset leads to stress and anger. A continual opportunity mindset leads to, well, continual opportunities.

When someone violates your rights, or when you perceive that someone violates your rights, you have at that moment a choice to make. You can see it as something happening *to* you. Or you can see it as something happening *for* you.

I wonder how quickly we could turn pain and regret into pleasure and power if we could only see that the thing that disappointed us—the job we lost, the person who left us, the misfortune that has haunted us—is actually a bridge to a better life, a better outcome. Intentional hurt can often become unintentional help.

Consider the story of Joseph in Genesis 37:18–36. His brothers, jealous and angry because they perceived that Joseph was their father's favorite, talked themselves out of murdering Joseph and had a moment of "compassion." Instead of killing him, they sold him into slavery.

By doing so, they thought they would get rid of the person who brought a bad report to their father about their efforts in the field; the tattletale; the snitch; the spoiled little brother with the coat of many colors. Selling Joseph into slavery would "right" the wrong they felt had been done to them. They would be free from the source of their displeasure and could divide the guilty gain. Their anger drove them to hate and betrayal. How big a forest such a little flame could burn!

There was no good that could come of this evil. Or was there?

You see, something strange happened on Joseph's way to slavery—he saved his world.

How? He made a decision. Not to look at life as something happening *to* him. Rather, he chose to look at life as something happening *for* him. Even what his brothers did somehow worked in his favor. Genesis 39:2 says, "The LORD was with Joseph, so he became a successful man."

Joseph had something that you and I can have, too—the right perspective. Every one of us is going to experience misfortune, disappointment, betrayal and rejection. But the way we look at it is going to shape the way we feel about it and therefore what we do about it.

This is what determines the outcome of our lives. It all starts with perspective. And when you factor God into any equation, it is much easier to adjust your perspective.

Notice the great results.

◈ Joseph, even though he lived in a foreign land, was continually promoted. He grew in power and influence just by serving faithfully wherever he ended up.

◈ Because of his gift of perspective, Joseph was asked to interpret one of Pharaoh's dreams. By doing so, he saved the lives of thousands of people, among them those of his own family—including Judah, from whose tribe Jesus descended.

◈ Joseph was the means by which God brought Israel into Egypt, where the Israelites developed as a people. The nation's deliverance resulted in a mighty display of divine power and gave birth to the concept of the Passover.

◈ Joseph became a foreshadowing of the Messiah—rejected, then elevated ("risen") to a high position, where he saved the world from starvation.

We do not always know what people are going to do to us. But God can overrule anything, resulting in the development of our character and power when it seems most unlikely.

As I like to say, what the enemy *sends* to defeat you, God *bends* to complete you.

Counting to ten is one thing, but anger only truly subsides from our lives when we gain perspective—when we see the bigger picture.

Joseph's brothers saw the little picture—their jealousy—so they became angry. Joseph, however, saw the big picture, so anger had no place to set up camp in him.

> What the enemy *sends* to defeat you, God *bends* to complete you.

What was the big picture he saw? While his brothers thought he would seek revenge against them in his newfound position as prime minister of Egypt, instead he shared with them the secret to his success and freedom from anger and bitterness: "But as for you, you meant evil against me; but God meant it for good, in order to bring it about as it is this day, to save many people alive" (Genesis 50:20 NKJV).

Notice the phrasing of this same verse in another translation: "You intended *to* harm me, but God intended it *for* good to accomplish what is now being done, the saving of many lives" (NIV, emphasis added).

This one perspective shift saved and changed the whole world. Instead of looking at life as something happening *to* him, Joseph looked at life as something happening *for* him and *for* the good of others. He believed that God was a turnaround specialist. He was right. And anything going in the wrong direction can turn around when you simply trust that God can rudely interrupt whatever the enemy sends to defeat you.

I call it a "but God" moment (see pages 30–31). Every one of us can have a "but God" moment. "Amazing grace! How sweet the sound that saved a wretch like me. I once was lost *but* now am found, was blind, *but* now I see."

This simple example is repeated over and over in the Bible and in life: "But God was with him" (Acts 7:9 ESV). "But God intended it for good" (Genesis 50:20 ISV). "But God was merciful!" (Ephesians 2:5 CEV).

Paul said, "God causes all things to work together *for* good" (Romans 8:28, emphasis added). Things are not just happening *to* us—they are happening *for* us. This is everything you need to calm your soul and build a life of confident peace.

You do not need a perfect environment to have perfect peace. Sometimes we wait before changing perspectives. We feel we have to get rid of all our enemies first. But God's Kingdom does not operate like that. Rather, He prepares a table *for* us in the presence of our enemies (see Psalm 23:5).

God could easily remove all your enemies, remove life's obstacles, remove the people who make you mad. But instead, He gives you peace in the midst of the storm. He confounds the troublemakers by letting them see that the results they hoped to achieve will not be possible. Why? Because you found God's peace, and your anger lost its mastery over you.

The Roots of Anger

Where did anger come from?

Look no further than our bloody ancestor Cain, who was warned in advance by God that anger was crouching at the door. The blood of his brother, Abel, still speaks (see Hebrews 11:4). And reminds us what anger can do.

The two sons of Adam and Eve both went to present their offerings to God. Abel brought to the Lord the first of his flock, an animal sacrifice. Cain, on the other hand, brought the fruit of the ground that he had cultivated (see Genesis 4).

As the story goes, God was pleased with Abel's sacrifice but not Cain's. Why? Because ever since Adam and Eve sinned, God had been shedding the blood of an animal as a substitute for their sin and covering their nakedness with animal skins (see Genesis 3:21).

So when Abel brought an animal sacrifice, it was pleasing to God because it showed that Abel knew he could not cleanse himself but was trusting God. He knew that a blood sacrifice was a symbol of forgiveness and grace.

But when Cain brought fruit from his field, it signified that Cain thought he could be pleasing to God through his own works and efforts. It showed that Cain did not value the blood offering God had been making in exchange for his sins. We find out later, in Leviticus, that without the shedding of blood, there is no forgiveness (see Leviticus 17:11; Hebrews 9:22). This was the justice system established by God.

So now we can see anger's dirty origin:

- Cain got angry because he did not feel right with God.
- He got angry because he compared himself to his brother.
- He got angry because he saw his brother as the problem.

So God reached out to Cain and said, "Why are you angry? And why is your face gloomy?" (Genesis 4:6).

But instead of answering the question and talking *upward* with God about his emotions, Cain went and talked *outward* to his brother and decided to take his problem to him. In fact, Cain saw his brother *as* the problem. So Cain lashed out at him in anger, committing the first murder in human history and ruining his own life forever.

Whenever we blame someone else for our own attitudes or failures, we become angry at that person and fail to address the real issue.

This started in verse 8, where it says, "And it happened that when they were in the field Cain rose up against his brother Abel and killed him." Why did Cain kill Abel? Because he did not answer the question, *Why am I angry?* He did not ask himself, *Why am I experiencing this emotion of anger?* When you skip the why, your emotions start controlling you rather than you controlling them. On the other hand, when you answer the whys in life, you will almost always get to the root of a problem and be able to solve it from there.

As we recognize the three things that caused anger in the first humans, we can come to grips with our own anger. Here is how:

1. *Know that you are pleasing to God.* Have faith in His Son's blood sacrifice for your sin.
2. *Embrace your journey—not someone else's.* Do not compare yourself to other people. It is unfair to them and unfair to you. It will always make you feel "less than."
3. *Realize that other people are not your problem.* When you start valuing your life because you are made in God's image, it will powerfully affect the way you look at other people, who are also made in His image. It will give you a whole new perspective on people and the things they do.
4. *Take your power back.* The power to respond and react is in your hands.

I often say that every negative emotion in our lives stems from a sense of powerlessness. If you feel powerless over your past, you feel guilt; if you feel powerless over your present, you feel depressed; if you feel powerless over your future, you feel afraid.

When you feel like your freedom has been taken away, you feel anger. When you feel powerless to do anything about your situation, you feel anger. When you feel like your rights have been violated, you feel anger.

This is what oppression is. It is the removal of a person's power or right to control his or her own life. Acts 10:38 says that Jesus was anointed with the Holy Spirit and power to heal all who were oppressed by the devil. The devil is always conspiring to oppress you.

We were created by God to be free. So the enemy's first priority is to rob us of the knowledge of our rights and freedoms as children of God.

Picture this: Our emotions are like children. And our mind is like the parent. One has to be in authority over the other. You cannot let your children dictate how the family is run. In other words, you cannot let emotions run your life. If you can get that picture, that image in your mind, everything will change. Children are beautiful, as are emotions, when they are under control. No one likes to see a child out of control in a grocery store, at school, at church or anywhere else. And when our emotions are out of control, it is the same thing. This is where the downward spiral of any individual life, family or society begins.

When we understand our power—our rights—we will eliminate the sense of powerlessness that lies at the root of negativity and negative emotions. I am not referring to human rights as defined by the government. I am referring to our rights as children of God. This is the power you have now.

Let's look at a few of the rights that the Word of God lays out for us (also see page 142).

◈ You have the right, the privilege, the freedom to be a child of God. "But as many as received Him, to them He gave the right to become children of God" (John 1:12). And all you have to do to exercise that right is receive Him.

◆ You have the right to walk in God's presence. "Let us therefore come boldly to the throne of grace, that we may obtain mercy and find grace to help in time of need" (Hebrews 4:16 NKJV).

◆ You have the right to experience God's favor. "Surely, LORD, you bless the righteous; you surround them with your favor as with a shield" (Psalm 5:12 NIV).

◆ You have the right to reign in life. "Those who receive the abundance of grace and the free gift of righteousness reign in life through the one man Jesus Christ" (Romans 5:17 RSV).

◆ You have the right to answered prayers. "A prayer of a righteous person . . . can accomplish much" (James 5:16).

◆ You have the right to be healed. "This dear woman, a daughter of Abraham, has been held in bondage by Satan for eighteen years. Isn't it right that she be released, even on the Sabbath?" (Luke 13:16 NLT).

◆ You have the right to be free from sin. "Sin shall no longer be your master, because you are not under the law, but under grace" (Romans 6:14 NIV).

◆ You have the right to get up when you have fallen. "A righteous man falls seven times, and rises again" (Proverbs 24:16 RSV).

◆ You have the right to be loved even as Jesus is loved. "You love my followers as much as you love me" (John 17:23 CEV).

These are just some of the rights you have as a child of God. And these rights are empowering.

When someone or something is trying to keep you down, you know you have the right to get back up. That is when anger loses its hold on you.

When someone hurts you or hates you, you can power past anger by remembering your right to the love of God. He will right every wrong. As I said earlier, what the enemy sends to defeat you, God bends to complete you. The understanding of your rights is what neutralizes tension and anger and prevents your mistreatment of other people.

You can defuse anger or any negative emotion by refusing to allow your circumstances to dictate your beliefs. Your underlying beliefs are what feed your emotional health—or sickness.

While Paul was in a Roman prison in AD 62, what did he do? He wrote the book of Philippians. In it, he talked more about gratitude and joy than he did in any other book he wrote. You see, the quality of his life, even in the least desirable circumstances, was shaped by his perspective. His beliefs did not change under trial. This brought what I call emotional freedom. "Do not be anxious about anything, but in every situation, by prayer and petition, with thanksgiving, present your requests to God. And the peace of God, which transcends all understanding, will guard your hearts and your minds in Christ Jesus" (Philippians 4:6–7 NIV).

So reread the section about gratitude on pages 94–96. Remember that the magic of gratitude is that it cancels out anger completely. In fact, you cannot be angry and grateful at the same time, just as you cannot be afraid or bitter or offended and grateful at the same time. So refuse to remain ungrateful, and your potential in life will be unlimited. What people have done *to* you will not matter because you are focused on what God has done *for* you.

> "And the peace of God, which transcends all understanding, will guard your hearts and your minds in Christ Jesus."

And whenever you begin to feel angry or ungrateful, shift your focus to God's ability to turn things around. Expect a "but God" moment.

Let's Change It Today

A soft answer turns away wrath.
Proverbs 15:1 NKJV

Where there is anger, there is usually hidden pain that needs to be healed. Use this "cheat sheet" to free yourself from the power of anger and take the first step in healing your pain.

1. Discover the power within you.

Remember that anger comes from a sense of powerlessness. When we feel powerless to change something, we get afraid, leading to anger. As it says in 2 Timothy 1:7, "God has not given us a spirit of fear, but of power and of love and of a sound mind" (NKJV). Meditate on this verse. You have power. We often think we will achieve something with an act of anger, but we never do. All anger produces is strife, hatred, retaliation, stress and sickness.

2. Listen carefully and speak slowly.

James 1:19 says, "Be quick to hear, slow to speak, and slow to anger." God gave us two ears and one mouth, which means that we are supposed to listen at least twice as much as we talk. But so many times in conversation, we are not listening to what other people are saying. Instead, we are thinking of what we are planning to say next. Learn the vocabulary of silence. The act of listening goes a long way in marriage, in raising children, in business and in our relationship with God. Listen closely and patiently before speaking. Follow this simple pattern, and anger will lose its grip.

3. Realize that anger does not work.

Anger does not produce or achieve anything. James 1:20 says, "A man's anger does not bring about the righteousness of God." So since anger cannot achieve righteousness, why get angry? I don't know about you, but when I buy something and discover that it does not work, I take it back. For example, if you had an employee who did not work, produce or achieve, you would fire that person, right?

In the same way, you can "fire" anger from your life. It's not working. It doesn't achieve what you need.

4. Deal with unresolved conflict.

Ephesians 4:26 says, "Do not let the sun go down on your anger." Make peace with whomever you have something against today. Don't wait for a feeling. Don't wait for them to apologize. Do not let it fester. You will be amazed at how much less anger you will feel.

5. Direct your anger where it belongs—at the devil.

Ephesians 4:27 says, "Do not give the devil an opportunity." The devil wants you to blame others for your anger. But realize that there is no one to blame but the devil himself. And like a Marine Corps sniper who just spotted the enemy, turn your full arsenal of weapons completely on him. Use your anger to resist the devil. Speak the Word with fervent conviction and eliminate his opportunity to operate in your life.

6. Get the bigger picture.

Often, the reason we get mad or afraid is that we only see a snapshot of what's really going on. As soon as anger comes, ask God to open your eyes to the big picture. He did it for Elisha's servant. He will do it for you (see 2 Kings 6:16–17).

DECIDE AND DECLARE

- I have God given rights that no one can take from me. And I am empowered by those rights.
- I am healing from the pain that has made me angry. I will not be controlled by it anymore.
- I am free from the fear underneath it all.
- I receive the gift of perspective to shift my emotions from anger to peace, from bitterness to forgiveness.
- No matter what others have done to me, I am expecting a "But God" moment in my life.

NOW PRAY THIS WITH ME

Father, I embrace Your Power in my life. I am not powerless, as I once thought. You have seated me with Jesus and given me the rights of a child of God. No matter who has violated my rights, You will turn it around. Open my eyes to see how much is for me rather than what is against me. Open my eyes to see things from heaven's point of view. Deliver me from anger by delivering me from my fears, in Jesus' name, Amen.

PART III

PARTING GIFTS
for the SOUL

13

Free at Last

The Secrets to Healing and Emotional Freedom

Let us therefore come boldly to the throne of grace, that we
may obtain mercy and find grace to help in time of need.

Hebrews 4:16 NKJV

As I sat down to write and rewrite this chapter, I struggled to
find the right words. Then I heard the still, small voice of
God in my heart: *Tell my people I want them healed and free.*
With those words, a Scripture immediately popped into my head:
"God anointed Jesus of Nazareth with the Holy Spirit and with power,
who went about doing good and healing all who were oppressed by
the devil, for God was with Him" (Acts 10:38 NKJV).

There is so much goodness to unpack in that verse, but before we do
that, I want you to know this: God wants you healed and free. Whatever
is sick, inside or outside; whatever has tied you up in knots or weighed
you down; whatever is not good in your life—God will heal it all.

The archenemy of your soul is the devil. While Jesus wants to do
you good, the devil wants to do you bad. While Jesus wants to heal you
everywhere you are hurting, the devil wants to hurt you everywhere he

can. While Jesus wants to set you free, the devil wants you imprisoned to anything that can control you.

You see, Jesus came to this world to do three things:

1. to seek and save the lost through His love-drenched death and resurrection;
2. to introduce you to the Father, putting your hand in His and connecting you to the Creator and lover of your soul;
3. to destroy the works of the devil.

And what are the works of the devil? Well, there are too many to list here, but essentially Jesus defines the devil as a thief that "comes to steal, kill, and destroy" (John 10:10 WEB). So anything that steals, kills, or destroys can be traced back to that old serpent. You do not have to be a *CSI* detective to figure this out.

So let's unpack that Bible verse and tap into the healing and freedom that God so willingly wants you to experience.

First, I want to talk about God's desire to heal you. The word for "healing" in this verse is the Greek *iōmenos*, derived from *iáomai*, which, according to *Thayer's Greek-English Lexicon of the New Testament*, means "to cure, heal, to make whole, to free from errors and sins."[1]

Whether it is mental, emotional, physical or spiritual, healing is God's idea and God's desire for you. Whether the healing flows from this book, a Bible verse, a moment of prayer, a medical prescription or a miracle touch from heaven itself, all healing is God's idea.

And from this verse, we see clearly that the cause of oppression is the devil. So again, my lightning-quick mind tells me, *God is good and the devil is bad!* Hey, now, *that* is some deep theology, right?

Look for the Good

Acts 10:38 says that Jesus went about "doing good." So I want to encourage you to expect good in your life. Expect God to do you good.

He cannot do you bad, because there is nothing bad about Him, and He does not have anything bad to share.

So many of us are expecting bad things to happen. In 2020, we experienced a pandemic, riots, violence and economic ups and downs. It became easy to brace ourselves for the worst.

> Expect God to do you good. He cannot do you bad, because there is nothing bad about Him.

It was such a bad year that I called my mother and asked her if the offer she made me when I was a kid was still on the table.

She answered, "What offer?"

"You remember," I said, "when you used to say, 'If you don't get your act together, I will slap you all the way into next year!'"

I am teasing, but boy, we sure could have used that in 2020.

God spoke to me in the worst moment of the 2020 pandemic. He said, *Look for the good, Son. Look for the good.* The bad stuff is so easy to find. But you gotta intentionally look for the good.

So I want to encourage you: If you are having a bad day, start looking for the good in it. It is there. Having a bad year? Start looking for the good. It is there. In a difficult period of trial? Look for the good. It is there.

Joseph said to his brothers, when they thought he would kill them for throwing him into a pit and selling him into slavery, "But as for you, you meant evil against me; but God meant it for good" (Genesis 50:20 NKJV).

Don't you love that "but God" interruption? Are you ready for a "but God" moment? A moment when God grabs hold of whatever the devil sends to defeat you and bends it to complete you?

In Acts 10:38, we find a specific kind of healing from oppression. "Healing all who were oppressed by the devil" could be translated as "healing and restoring all those who have been pressed down by the spirit of violence and accusation."

Oppression is the worst enemy of our souls. It chokes the life out of us because its power lies in undermining our freedom. The greatest freedom we are given in life is to be free from oppression.

The Greek word for "oppressed" in this verse is *katadynasteuomenous*. According to Strong's *Exhaustive Concordance of the Bible*, it comes from the root words *kata*, meaning "down" or "against," and *dunastés*, meaning "ruler" or "potentate." In other words, an oppressed person is tyrannized, dominated by a ruler, kept down. This shows us the dark underbelly of the devil and his efforts to destroy your soul by finding a way to keep you down.

The devil is actively working to oppress you. He wants to (1) powerfully bring you down, (2) deny you the high position and blessings you should enjoy, and (3) tyrannize, dominate and treat you harshly. In other words, he wants you powerless in life.

Remember that oppression means to deny a person's power to control his or her own life and future. Jesus, on the other hand, came to set people free and give them their power back. He said, "The Spirit of the Lord . . . has sent me to proclaim liberty to captives . . . [and] to let the oppressed go free" (Luke 4:18 NABRE).

Something Is Broken Inside

Jesus wants to heal you from the oppression weighing down on you and pickpocketing your power. He wants to help you regain your ability to love. He wants to restore your sound mind. He wants to remove whatever has pressed so hard against you that it broke something inside.

The will to go on, the will to overcome, the will to break barriers—all this has been broken by the weight of stress, anxiety or a poor self-image. And Jesus wants to heal it all.

Isaiah paints a beautiful picture of the Messiah before He arrived on the scene. God gave the prophet insight into how powerful Jesus' healing touch would be: *"He won't brush aside the bruised and the hurt and he won't disregard the small and insignificant, but he'll steadily and firmly set things right. He won't tire out and quit. He won't be stopped until he's finished his work—to set things right on earth*" (Isaiah 42:4 MSG).

Martin Luther said, "He does not cast away, nor crush, nor condemn the wounded in conscience, those who are terrified in view of their sins; the weak in faith and practice, but watches over and cherishes them, makes them whole, and affectionately embraces them."[2]

What is hurting you today? Where is your pain?

Life has crushed us; it has wounded us all. We have been wounded by the oppression of illness, the oppression of a broken heart, the oppression of rejection. But Jesus will make us whole.

What love! What a beautiful Savior, always ready to bestow His healing touch, which He so willingly wants to give.

Jesus lavished His compassion and mercy on all who asked for it. His healing was a merciful act of God toward the sick, oppressed and pained. Below are just a few examples from the Bible.

The Two Blind Men

"As Jesus went on from there, two blind men followed him, crying loudly, '*Have mercy on us,* Son of David!' . . . And their eyes were opened" (Matthew 9:27, 30 NRSV, emphasis added).

The Demon-Possessed Child

"Just then a Canaanite woman from that region came out and started shouting, '*Have mercy on me,* Lord, Son of David; my daughter is tormented by a demon.' . . . And her daughter was healed instantly" (15:22, 28 NRSV, emphasis added).

The Epileptic Son

"A man came to him, knelt before him, and said, 'Lord, *have mercy on my son,* for he is an epileptic and he suffers terribly; he often falls into the fire and often into the water.' . . . And the boy was cured instantly" (17:14–15, 18 NRSV, emphasis added).

Two More Blind Men

"There were two blind men sitting by the roadside. When they heard that Jesus was passing by, they shouted, 'Lord, *have mercy on us,* Son of David!' The crowd sternly ordered them to be quiet; but they shouted even more loudly, *'Have mercy on us,* Lord, Son of David!' . . . Immediately they regained their sight" (20:30–31, 34 NRSV, emphasis added).

The Gerasene Demoniac

"Jesus . . . said to him, 'Go home to your friends, and tell them how much the Lord has done for you, and what *mercy* he has shown you'" (Mark 5:19 NRSV, emphasis added).

Blind Bartimaeus

"When he heard that it was Jesus of Nazareth, he began to shout out and say, 'Jesus, Son of David, *have mercy on me!'* Many sternly ordered him to be quiet, but he cried out even more loudly, 'Son of David, *have mercy on me!'* . . . Immediately he regained his sight" (10:47–48, 52 NRSV, emphasis added).

The Ten Lepers

"As [Jesus] entered a village, ten lepers approached him. Keeping their distance, they called out, saying, 'Jesus, Master, *have mercy on us!'* . . . and as they went, they were made clean" (Luke 17:12–14 NRSV, emphasis added).

Notice the thing that all those who were healed had in common: They all said, "Have mercy on me." And notice what else they had in common: Every one of them was healed or set free.

Healing and freedom from pain starts with mercy. There is not enough counseling or medicine or positive thinking out there to heal some of our deepest pain and oppression. But there is plenty of mercy.

Let's Go to Him Now

Why not take a moment right now and ask Jesus for mercy? Why not ask him to heal you or show mercy and heal a loved one in your life?

Let's pray together: "Jesus, You are full of mercy, and there is mercy at your throne. So I am asking for healing and freedom where I am hurting and oppressed. And I thank you for your healing and deliverance."

Now believe you have received it.

Jesus said, "Ask and you will receive, so that your joy may be made full" (John 16:24).

Mercy is the divine urge to relieve people of the suffering or pain that they are in. And it is not in short supply: "Let us therefore come boldly to the throne of grace, that we may obtain mercy and find grace to help in time of need" (Hebrews 4:16 NKJV).

> "Ask and you will receive, so that your joy may be made full."

Notice how this is written in *The Message*: "So let's walk right up to him and get what he is so ready to give. Take the mercy, accept the help."

God is seated on a throne of grace. It is not a throne of judgment for His children. It is a throne of grace. It is a place we can go to in prayer and ask for mercy and help in our time of need. And He is *so* ready to dispense it in abundance to whoever asks.

Let's look more closely at the ten lepers who were cleansed. In Jesus' time, leprosy was considered the worst possible disease and curse anyone could experience. Previously, we read about the one leper who turned back to thank Jesus. But I want to show you something else amazing in this story.

"As [Jesus] entered a village, ten lepers approached him. Keeping their distance, they called out, saying, 'Jesus, Master, have mercy on us!' When he saw them, he said to them, 'Go and show yourselves to the priests.' And as they went, they were made clean" (Luke 17:12–14 NRSV).

Notice that the lepers asked for mercy. And what happened next? "He saw them."

The point I want to make here is that as soon as the lepers asked for mercy, they had Jesus' attention. God gives His attention to anyone who appeals to Him for mercy.

I want you to understand three powerful truths from the miracle Jesus performed: (1) God sees you in your pain; (2) God will speak to you in your pain; (3) God will heal your pain.

This is where so many people miss the healing and freedom right in front of them. We are waiting for something miraculous to happen in our lives. We are waiting to see it all before we move. But it is in the *movement*, the next step, that we find His strength.

Remember when Jesus was in the Garden of Gethsemane? Remember that in His weakest moment, with the weight of the world's sin on His shoulders, "He went forward a little" (Mark 14:35 kjv)? So often it is just one small step that will catapult us into our healing and deliverance.

Maybe it is the step of asking for mercy. Maybe it is the step of speaking God's Word or thanking Him in advance or forgiving yourself for something you have done.

Jesus "knelt down and prayed, 'Father, if You are willing, take this cup from Me. Yet not My will, but Yours be done.' Then an angel from heaven appeared to Him and strengthened Him" (Luke 22:41–43 bsb).

Wow! Notice how supernatural strength came to Jesus: He moved forward a little. He surrendered His will to God's will. Then an angel strengthened Him.

This Greek word for "strengthened" in this passage is *enischuó*. It means "being strong enough to face necessary confrontation."

When we just take one step forward, God's grace meets us there. God's strength meets us as we simply open our mouths or lift up our hands or begin to pray; as we invite God to do His will, strength comes. Angels come. Power comes. Heaven backs us up with a full supply of strength to face whatever we are dealing with.

Jesus' Healing Power in YOU

Now let's talk about the three areas of our lives that Jesus brings His healing power to.

1. He heals us of sickness and disease.

"And if the Spirit of him who raised Jesus from the dead is living in you, he who raised Christ from the dead will also give life to your mortal bodies" (Romans 8:11 NIV). "And Jesus went about all the cities and villages, teaching in their synagogues, and preaching the gospel of the kingdom, and healing every sickness and every disease among the people" (Matthew 9:35 KJV).

Jesus has not changed. He is the same yesterday, today and forever. If He healed yesterday, He can heal today. Ask for and expect His healing touch for any sickness or disease you may be experiencing.

2. He heals us of heartbreak.

The heart is the seat of all affection. It is the home of feelings and emotions. It is the soil where the dreams God wants to give us can grow. But it is also the soil where wounds take root.

Remember that wherever there is anger, there are usually hidden wounds that need to be healed. The good news is that healing is here: "He heals the brokenhearted and binds up their wounds" (Psalm 147:3 ESV). Jesus said, "The Spirit of the LORD is upon Me, because He has anointed Me to preach the gospel to the poor; He has sent Me to heal the brokenhearted" (Luke 4:18 NKJV).

> "He has sent Me to heal the brokenhearted."

Every one of us at one time or another experiences the pain of a broken heart.

As I wrote above, a broken heart cannot contain the dreams, the hopes, the ideas, the destinies and the great things God created us for. If the heart is broken, the dreams spill out. And when the heart is broken, all we try to do is keep filling it with things that dull the pain.

But no matter who or what caused your heartbreak, Jesus will heal it. Isaiah 42:3 says, "A bruised reed he will not break" (NIV).

3. He heals us of the past.

So many of us have been limited, oppressed and rendered powerless by the past. We have been held captive by our mistakes, our weaknesses. Well, God has a remedy for that.

When the Holy Spirit gets involved in our lives, He heals us of *who we used to be*. If we were weak, He can make us strong. If we were shy, He can make us bold. If we were depressed, He can make us rejoice. If we felt useless, He can give us purpose.

> "If anyone is in Christ, he is a new creation."

So often we relate to people based on who they were when we met them. But God does not see us like that. Scripture says, "If anyone is in Christ, he is a new creation; old things have passed away, and look, new things have come" (2 Corinthians 5:17 HCSB). What an amazing promise! Let's take God at His word. Let's open ourselves to the Spirit of God's healing and allow Him to change us into the people He intended us to be.

When God heals you of your past, He frees you from

- ◈ who you used to be
- ◈ addictions you used to have
- ◈ prejudices you used to carry
- ◈ legalism (or religious rigidity)

Legalistic views of God and unrealistic expectations of ourselves and others afflict countless people. And it is something I suffered from and inflicted on others for many years as a believer. I may have known God's unmerited grace when I first accepted Jesus, but so often we get so focused on what we must "do for God" that we forget that all the good happens when we focus on what God has *done* for us, through the free gift of Jesus and the Holy Spirit.

Thomas L. Schreiner, a biblical scholar and professor at Southern Baptist Theological Seminary, tells us that "legalism exists when people attempt to secure righteousness in God's sight by good works. Legalists believe that they can earn or merit God's approval by performing the requirements of the law."[3] But no one can perform all the requirements of the old covenant laws. The commandments actually prove how desperately we need a Savior, because in one sense we are all guilty. But in another sense, that's why Jesus went to the Cross, to wash away our guilt and shame. The Christianity of the Cross is not a religion. It is a demonstration of love and a call to be loved and to love. There is no freedom in strapping ourselves to religious rituals and requirements we cannot fully fulfill. Our excessive compulsion to be holy enough will never be enough. Religion that restricts free choice and makes us rigid, harsh, self-righteous and judgmental is too much to bear. It makes us feel like we're in a spiritual straitjacket, with no room to freely move, live and breathe, as we were designed by God to do. As Paul tells us, "Where the Spirit of the Lord is, there is freedom" (2 Corinthians 3:17 CSB).

This excessive conformity to the law, forced upon us by judgmental leaders and demonic thoughts, is what is choking believers worldwide and vandalizing the beauty of Jesus and His Church.

God does not come into our lives from the outside, through religious rigidity and rules. He works within us, by His Holy Spirit: "But we all, with unveiled face, beholding as in a mirror the glory of the Lord, are being transformed into the same image from glory to glory, just as from the Lord, the Spirit" (2 Corinthians 3:18 NASB1995).

There is something very powerful about inviting the Holy Spirit to move in your life.

Recall what happened when the Spirit of the Lord came upon Samson (yes, *that* Samson—as in Samson and Delilah). Some people mistakenly think Samson was naturally strong. But it was the Spirit of God that transformed him from an average man to a supernatural man: "At that moment the Spirit of the LORD came powerfully upon him, and he ripped the lion's jaws apart with his bare hands. He did it as easily as if it were a young goat. But he didn't tell his father or mother about it" (Judges 14:6 NLT).

Wow! Are you ready to become a man or woman who rips lions apart? Are you ready to be healed from who you used to be? That's exactly what happened to Samson. And that is exactly what will happen to you. (Umm . . . just leave those lions alone, though. They are cool, and they are not bothering you.)

Here is yet another example of the way the Holy Spirit heals you of *who you used to be*. As Samuel told King Saul in the Old Testament, "The Spirit of the LORD will come upon you mightily, and you shall prophesy with them and be changed into another man" (1 Samuel 10:6 NASB1995). The story continues in verses 9–11 (NASB1995):

> Then it happened when [Saul] turned his back to leave Samuel, God changed his heart; and all those signs came about on that day. When they came to the hill there, behold, a group of prophets met him; and the Spirit of God came upon him mightily, so that he prophesied among them. It came about, when all who knew him previously saw that he prophesied now with the prophets, that the people said to one another, "What has happened to the son of Kish? Is Saul also among the prophets?"

Notice, it was God who changed Saul's heart. He became a different man, because God's Spirit came mightily upon him.

Realize that God can do the same thing for you. He can heal you of who you used to be and can turn you into the person you were meant to be.

He did it for Samson. He did it for Saul.

He did it for Peter. He did it for Paul.

You are not forgotten. He will do it for *all*.

DECIDE AND DECLARE

- ◈ Today is my healing day.
- ◈ I will no longer be oppressed by the devil, by people or by anything in life.
- ◈ I am no longer a slave to my past, my pain, my prejudices.
- ◈ I am free from religious legalism and self-righteousness.
- ◈ I am free to be the best version of myself beginning today.

NOW PRAY THIS WITH ME

Holy Spirit, today I invite You to heal me. You are healing me of disease, You are healing me of brokenheartedness, and You are healing me of who I used to be. It's not too late for me to become who I could have been before the damage was done in my life. There's an anointing in my life and in this book to do me good and heal me everywhere I'm hurting. I thank You for all this and more in the name of Jesus, Amen.

14

How to Stop Feeling Bad and Start Enjoying Life

> The thief comes only to steal and kill and destroy; I have
> come that they may have life, and have it to the full.
>
> John 10:10 NIV

I don't know when feeling bad about ourselves became so popular. But I would like to make it unpopular for you by the time this chapter is through.

You know you are a pretty good person. You may even think you are a great person—just ask your mother! You even take pretty good selfies (after a few . . . hundred tries).

But there is a different recording playing inside your head. *You're not good enough. You haven't done enough. You should feel bad for what you thought, for what you did, for what you did not do*—and on and on, that familiar voice tells you.

Some religions will scold us. Feeling bad enough is the path to feeling good, they say. Family members might reinforce that idea, and our old archenemy will try to shame us with how bad we should feel about ourselves.

But there is no such thing as perfect, except God. And when you are born again, you are considered righteous and holy in God's eyes.

In other people's eyes, you will not ever look or act perfect, but that is why you need to experience freedom from "people bondage." That's the fear of what people will say or think about you. So often, the reason we feel worthless is because we are enslaved by the opinions of others, good and bad.

As we get wiser (sometimes that comes from getting older; sometimes it comes from getting burned), and as we mature in life, we lose interest in being held captive to other people's thoughts about us.

It kind of follows this progression: When we are 25, we are very concerned with what people think about us. When we are 45, we do not care as much about what people think about us. But when we are 75, we realize that *no one is thinking about us.* Funny, but pretty accurate!

Jesus said something very powerful that has helped me greatly in this: "I'm not interested in crowd approval" (John 5:41 MSG). In another translation, He said: "I am not looking for human praise" (GNT). And my favorite translation: "Your approval means nothing to me" (NLT).

This is such a liberating truth for our hearts to hear. Jesus did not live for the approval of other people. Why? Besides the fact that He was the Son of God, He also had a deep, abiding understanding of God's love and approval of Him as a man.

When He was thirty years old, He allowed Himself to be baptized by His cousin John the Baptist. John was hesitant about baptizing someone he knew was greater than he was—someone whose sandals he said he was "not worthy to untie" (Luke 3:16 ESV).

But Jesus insisted, saying, "Permit it . . . to fulfill all righteousness" (Matthew 3:15 NKJV). He did not need to be baptized, because He had never sinned, but He wanted to fulfill all the requirements of God's law so He could be the perfect sacrifice for us.

And as He came up from the waters of baptism, "a voice from heaven said, 'You are my dearly loved Son, and you bring me great joy'" (Mark

1:11 NLT). Other translations say, "in You I am well-pleased" (AMP), "I am pleased with you" (CEV), and "in you I take great delight" (NET).

Notice how personal and powerful these words from the Most High—our heavenly Father—are. They meet the deepest human need we have: love and acceptance, approval and affirmation.

Notice, too, that God approved of Jesus before He performed a miracle and before He made the ultimate sacrifice, dying for our sins. Therefore, God's approval and delight did not come from anything Jesus did. Rather, it came simply from from the fact that Jesus was His Son. And that approval was enough for Jesus.

We, too, are sons and daughters of God when we receive Jesus as our Savior. And we, too—*you*, too—bring our heavenly Father great joy just for being His.

> God's approval and delight did not come from anything Jesus did. Rather, it came simply from from the fact that Jesus was His Son.

I know it is hard to believe, but the authentic Gospel of God's unfailing grace and love has been vandalized by religion. God's beautiful smile of affection and approval has had graffiti spray-painted all over it, creating a distorted view of His head-over-heels affection for you. And who are the vandals? Religious leaders who insist on painting a picture of an angry God who will wipe you off the face of the planet if you do not fall in line.

This distortion lies at the root of why we feel bad about ourselves. We lack confidence in God's approval—the basis for feeling right and good and happy and healthy in life. This is why people crave approval. This is what undermines your perception of your own worth, your true value and your true potential.

By wasting energy on finding approval, we lose the energy necessary to build our lives and destiny upon the seal of God's approval from day one. This turns people into approval addicts—approvaholics.

You may argue, *But Jesus was perfect. We're not like Him. So we do not have the same approval from the Father as He had.* Oh, really?

Then why does Scripture say, "As Jesus is, so also are we in this world" (1 John 4:17 NET)?

By receiving Jesus' blood sacrifice for us, we become God's family. We are of the same blood. Washed and redeemed by Him. He becomes our Abba, Father. Our daddy God.

And how does He feel about you? He is celebrating you! He is singing because of you: "The Lord your God wins victory after victory and is always with you. He celebrates and sings because of you, and he will refresh your life with his love" (Zephaniah 3:17 CEV). He is smiling at you: "You'll see God's smile and celebrate, finding yourself set right with God" (Job 33:26 MSG).

This powerful truth of God's love and approval of you will set you free from fear. This is what makes it so easy to run to Him in our time of need, or any time at all. He is the everlasting Father whose arms we can lean on and fall into.

In fact, whenever I have felt afraid, I have leaned on these enduring truths: "I cried to him and he answered me! He freed me from all my fears" (Psalm 34:4 TLB).

So many people are filled with sadness and fear, simply because they are seeking approval, acceptance and confidence in what other people think about them. This fear and sadness prevents them from having healthy relationships.

You can be totally free from this fear. Just follow these simple steps.

- Ask God to free you from your fear today. He will.
- Be convinced of His love for you.
- Whenever your fear comes, pray for the person you feel fearful of, or pray for boldness and give that fear to God.
- Look for a way to encourage another person. There is always someone who needs a pat on the back, an attaboy or a kind word or gesture.
- Never take the advice of your fears. Let love lead you. And lead with love.

How to Enjoy Your Life

The chains of your past are broken and gone, but the devil does not want you to realize that. He is the accuser (see Revelation 12:10), the one who continually holds you down in a never-ending cycle of shame, blame, finger-pointing and accusations.

His narrative goes something like this: *You won't change. You're not really forgiven. You cannot come back from this—at least not completely. God won't use you now. You're damaged goods. You'll never be trustworthy again. Your life is ruined. You are nothing. You are guilty. End of story.*

But the way to silence the accuser's voice forever is to notice the weapon he uses against you: bad thinking. This means wrong thinking—negative thoughts that accuse, limit, criticize, defeat and condemn you.

If you want to change how you feel, it starts by changing how you think. And changing how you think starts by changing what you feed your mind. What we feed our minds comes from who we surround ourselves with and what goes into our eyes and ears—if you feed your soul the modern-day news, you will live a life of fear. Our eyes and ears are the gateway to the soul. And we should be filling them with the good news of God's promises, along with the beauty He has created in the world around us.

The archenemy also has another weapon—he attacks the heart. He infiltrates it with lies that sound right. But God's Word gives us the key to defeating this attack: "Watch over your heart with all diligence, for from it flow the springs of life" (Proverbs 4:23 AMP).

The water fountains and wells in the Middle East at the time the Scriptures were written had to be watched with extraordinary care to prevent the contamination or poisoning of the source of life for so many. The heart is just such a fountain and should be guarded no less carefully. All "springs" flow from one fountainhead. How vital, then, to guard the heart. We guard our family, property and health, and rightly so, but the heart should be guarded all the more, for as a man "thinks

214

in his heart, so is he" (Proverbs 23:7 NKJV). You see? The heart *is* the man! The heart *is* the woman!

⁓

I struggled for years with depression and anxiety. During those periods, I felt like there was something wrong with me, something different about me. I felt like I was being punished with those feelings, until I realized that they are just feelings, just emotions. They are not anything more than that. They are meant to be felt, but not meant to be in charge.

I also felt guilty if I felt good! So I felt bad for feeling good, which made me feel bad! See the cycle? I felt it was wrong to enjoy life. Because after all, enjoying life seemed selfish, until I tapped into the power of this verse: "Instruct those who are rich in the present age not to be arrogant or to set their hope on the uncertainty of wealth, but on God, who richly provides us with all things to enjoy" (1 Timothy 6:17 HCSB).

Now, there is a lot to be said about trusting God and not the uncertainty of riches, but the emphasis I want to place in this verse is on the word *enjoy.*

God supplies us with all things to enjoy. God is interested in our enjoyment of the things He has made and given us. Enjoyment is God's idea.

Enjoyment is God's idea.

The Garden of Eden was the first proof of God's intention for humankind. When He created Adam and Eve, he put them in Eden. The English word *eden* comes from the Hebrew word *ēdhen*, which shares roots with the Hebrew word *ednah*, meaning "pleasure." It was the garden of pleasure.

And in Psalms, we can see again that pleasure is God's idea: "In Your presence is fullness of joy; at Your right hand are pleasures forevermore" (Psalm 16:11 NKJV).

Now, there are many things that people use to manufacture temporary pleasure. Even sin is "pleasurable" for a time, as the Bible tells us. But true pleasure, true enjoyment, comes from God.

Let's go back to 1 Timothy 6:17: God "richly provides us with all things to enjoy" (HCSB).

There is a fascinating word that God tucks into this verse. The Greek word for "enjoy" is *apolausin*, which also forms the root of the word *applause*. When we enjoy a concert, sporting event or just an immensely pleasurable moment, we applaud.

God, being the loving Father and Creator that He is, wants to flood our lives with moments that we will be able to applaud. Religious distortions of God's intention have sabotaged our expectations and hijacked the true concept of God. He is not a 24-hour-a-day inspector of your life, actions and motives. He is not going to strike out at you if you get out of line or have fun.

Pleasure, happiness and fun were all God's ideas. He does not expect you or want you to purge your life of enjoyment. There is nothing holy about that. Extreme forms of self-denial often lead to self-hate or self-harm.

The biblical model of self-denial is based on denying the belief systems that defeat you: denying your opinions in favor of God's opinions and denying your own efforts to satisfy God's righteousness, and instead glorifying Jesus' substitutionary sacrifice on the cross. This is truly "denying self."

People who try to rid their lives of the enjoyment and pleasure God intended for us usually suppress their true feelings and desires until they leak out over time or burst out in some perverted or twisted way.

If we suppress all sexual urges, for example, thinking that we are pleasing God by doing so, those urges can find unhealthy outlets, such as pornography addiction or the objectifying of other human beings. Sexual desire is beautiful and godly, not demonic and evil.

The way in which we express and fulfill our desires determines whether they are good or bad. I believe that when we follow the recipe for enjoyment that I lay out here, it will satisfy the true needs of the soul. Then discerning between good and bad in sexuality can be accomplished from a healthy place rather than from the overflow of what I call soul sickness.

Emotional damage and self-abuse come from trying to "sanitize" our lives. Somehow, Christian culture has taken a wrong turn in this regard and fallen into a ditch.

One ditch on the road to a healthy soul is total abstinence—refraining from any kind of enjoyment whatsoever. The other ditch is hedonism—going all in on the pleasures of this world. Neither of these extremes is healthy.

We have to be intentional in our pursuit of a life of freedom and enjoyment. "Abstainers" insist that if you are enjoying your life too much, you are being unspiritual and not heavenly minded. Abstainers also suffer greatly when they fail. Because they regard purity as the measure of their health and relationship with God, they beat themselves up when they fall short of that ideal. Self-condemnation becomes their penance and leaves them continually unhappy.

I should know. I existed that way for many years as a Christian, constantly trying to live up to a standard so high that any infraction brought me guilt and self-abasement and made me critical of myself and others.

On the other hand, extreme pleasure seekers are willing to pursue their happiness at other people's expense. They get so focused on themselves that they become takers and miss out on the joy and happiness that come from giving and serving others. Because they are driven by the things that hit the pleasure center of their brains, they often find themselves needing a bigger fix each time—something newer and more pleasurable than what they had before. Gratitude is in short supply for people focused on themselves.

Where do we find the balance? How do we strike the right chord in our souls?

Well, we have to start by giving ourselves permission to enjoy our lives in spite of all the reasons the enemy will give us to be miserable.

A Recipe for Enjoying Life

My recipe for enjoying life starts with the Bible verse I mentioned on page 215: "Instruct those who are rich in the present age not to be arrogant or to set their hope on the uncertainty of wealth, but on God, who richly provides us with all things to enjoy" (1 Timothy 6:17 CSB). Then add the following ingredients.

◈ *Aim your hope in the right direction.* When your hope is in God, you find meaning and satisfaction. What do I mean by putting hope in God? I mean stop making your relationship with God revolve around your faithfulness and your ability to check all the boxes. Instead, put your hope in *His* faithfulness. Build your life around the promises He makes to you rather than the promises you make to Him.

◈ *Don't be conceited.* Pride and self-centeredness bring misery. Humility brings enjoyment and happiness. Being down-to-earth rather than keeping your nose in the air will bring enjoyment.

◈ *Believe that God "richly provides."* Rid yourself of the idea or "idol" of a stingy God. Which part of "richly provides" do you not understand? God is in the supply business. He supplies us with all things to enjoy. Enjoyment is God's idea. He does not want your existence to be boring, empty or ascetic. Jesus said, "I came that they may have and enjoy life, and have it in abundance (to the full, till it overflows)" (John 10:10 AMPC).

Remember what I said in the opening section of this book? Of course not! That's why I am going to say it again. "God keeps such people so busy enjoying life that they take no time to brood over the past" (Ecclesiastes 5:20 NLT).

This is what is going to happen to you. God is gonna keep you so busy enjoying life that you will not live in your past regrets, shame or failures. I love how this verse is written in the New International Version: "They seldom reflect on the days of their life, because God keeps them occupied with gladness of heart." The present gladness God wants to give you will so fill your heart that you can hardly even remember the pain and regret of the past.

And as an exclamation point, I offer these tips and invite you to give yourself permission to indulge in them all.

◈ *Enjoy your relationship with God.* Remember that we can enjoy our relationship with God when we stop making it about our faithfulness to Him and focus on His faithfulness to us. For "if we are faithless, He remains faithful" (2 Timothy 2:13). This is liberating intel from God.

◈ *Enjoy your self.* Do not make life about finding a mate, matey! (Insert pirate-voice "Arggghhh" here.) When we wait for another person to complete our happiness, we are wasting precious time. Learn to enjoy the quiet, the moments of alone time with God. People will disappoint you. Life will disappoint you. The world supplies enough disappointment. Stop piling on! When you enjoy your own company, you become a magnetic force, drawing others into your circle of enjoyment. You attract the right people and you repel wrong ones.

◈ *Enjoy your family.* Recognize that family life is simply dysfunction waiting to happen. Be self-effacing. Have fun with your family rather than being ashamed of them. They may have put the *dys* in *dysfunction*, but no one has it all together. We are all a work in progress. So relax and look for the good in your family members.

◈ *Enjoy your relationships with people.* Limit what you expect of people and start seeing them as sources of enjoyment rather than as suppliers of something you need. The way we see people changes everything: "I thank God every time I remember you" (Philippians 1:3 ERV). See people not as problems to solve but as pleasures to enjoy. Does a "problem" person come to your mind, right now, as you are reading this? Stop and thank God for that person. As you remember the people who have brought good into you life, it will make you thankful.

◈ *Enjoy your church.* Nothing brings enjoyment like being in a healthy community of believers, connecting with them closely and often, and giving back to the work of the community's mission. "Speak to one another with psalms, hymns and songs from the Spirit. Sing and make music from your heart to the Lord. Always give thanks to God the Father for everything. Give thanks to him in the name of our Lord Jesus Christ" (Ephesians 5:19–20 NIRV). Notice how celebratory the Church is supposed to be. Yet too often it has become a place known for taking the fun out of life, or shaming you for having too much fun, rather than being, as it should, a source of celebration and joy. Enjoy the power of agreement that comes from a church that prays with you and for you. And enjoy the camaraderie, the power, the miracles, the simplicity of communion, the good news that is constantly shared. The blessings of a church are too many to count. (If you do not have a church you enjoy, connect with me at LifeChangersGlobal.com.)

◆ *Enjoy your body.* Stop hating and shaming your body. Realize that God made you and chose to live inside you. For years, so many believers have misunderstood God's Word about the human body. Scripture says, "Your body is the temple of the Holy Spirit" (1 Corinthians 6:19 JUB). And it is true: It is. But this Scripture is not a warning to never do anything bad or "God'll getcha." Through this verse, God is revealing to us our incomparable worth to Him. God could live anywhere He wants. And yet He chose to live inside of you. What value you have to Him!

Time to Eat

I cannot end this chapter without urging you to give yourself permission to enjoy your food. (Food could be the subject of a chapter or book on its own, but I am tucking it in here to help you experience a "taste" of real freedom in this area as soon as possible.)

Food is one of my favorite topics. And there is a lot to say because so many people have a messed-up relationship with food. And what I am about to say may seem controversial—or it could set you free.

Food is meant to be enjoyed. Not withheld.

Depriving yourself of foods you enjoy is unhealthy and often leads to binge eating.

Telling yourself that certain foods are off-limits actually gives them power over you. It gives them a certain allure that they would not have otherwise.

Anyone who has ever tried to lose weight knows how it goes: Feel bad about your diet, then throw out all the "bad" foods—the evil harlots called pizza, pasta and brownies—and then become best friends with turkey breast and tofu.

But sooner or later we give in to our urges, then promise ourselves that we will never eat those tempting foods again. Rinse and repeat.

I'm not suggesting that we ignore the risks of heart disease, obesity and diabetes associated with overeating, because those conditions are already at epidemic levels in our society. Why? Because people are lazy and unintelligent? I don't believe that at all.

The root problem is the absence of a sense of value and purpose. Couple that with the glorification of weight loss and the emotional stigma it inflicts and you have a recipe for a terrible relationship with food.

We do need to seek and guard good health. But that starts with a healthy soul, which turns into a healthy relationship with food.

And by the way, whose idea was it to enjoy food in a healthful way, anyway? Hmm . . . let's see: "Out of the ground the LORD God made to spring up every tree that is pleasant to the sight and good for food. The tree of life was in the midst of the garden, and the tree of the knowledge of good and evil" (Genesis 2:9 ESV). And "the LORD God commanded the man, saying, 'From any tree of the garden you may eat freely'" (Genesis 2:16 NASB 1995).

Notice that God's command was not about what *not* to eat. It was about what *to* eat. This set me free when I realized this.

Unfortunately, the diet industry has not absorbed the lesson of this verse. Maybe they do not know it is there. But I do, and I am sharing it with you.

I believe the "health" industry has focused on the allure of weight loss rather than on the health and well-being of the soul. And why is that? Because it sells. In fact, according to the Global Wellness Institute, the global health and wellness industry is worth $4.2 *trillion*.[1] Why fix what ain't broke? But the problem is, our souls and bodies are broken, and that is what needs to be fixed. Once the soul gets well, the whole gets well.

Furthermore, depriving yourself of foods you enjoy is stressful. And almost always leads to binge eating. More importantly, it can lead to depression and a downward spiral of emotions and self-defeating mindsets and behaviors.

What I have discovered (why it took me decades I have no idea) is that the best diet is no diet. I am not encouraging you to eat everything in sight. You do not want to be the person in the seafood joke—the one who, in response to the question "Do you like seafood?" answers, "Yes. Whenever I see food, I eat it."

I have found it far more liberating to identify a reasonable number of calories that corresponds to the number of calories I burn and try to stick to it. I always include at least one meal I love or one special treat I love per day. I just make sure it is counted in my daily calorie total.

For example, if you love Klondike bars (as I do), allow yourself one each evening or three or four times a week and make the process of eating it an enjoyable, guilt-free experience, something you share with God. I am pretty sure He loves Klondike bars, too! They are divine. 😄

By giving yourself permission to eat the things you enjoy, cravings lose their power over your emotions. When your emotions are ruled by cravings, you develop a damaged relationship with food, people and even yourself, which is a precursor to bad choices.

God is primarily interested in the health of our souls. Instead of associating our favorite foods with sin and gluttony, we should associate them with God's blessings and the fact that He "richly provides us with all things to enjoy." Let's adopt a mentality of moderation rather than shaming ourselves with guilt and depression for craving what's good.

Food is designed by God to be connected to our emotions. He wants us to associate good foods with a life of celebration. That is why we read in the Bible, "Bring the fattened calf" (Luke 15:23), "The Son of Man came eating and drinking" (Matthew 11:19), and "I have come down to rescue them . . . and bring them up . . . to a land flowing with milk and honey" (Exodus 3:8).

Jesus' first miracle was turning water into wine at a wedding; His final moments with His disciples were spent at the Last Supper with bread and wine. Food is intertwined with great memories and celebrations in most of our lives. To deliberately and continually deprive ourselves of pleasurable foods leads to sadness and a feeling of being punished. Nobody should feel that. That is why I believe in having a healthy relationship with food, one in which you can enjoy your favorite things in a measured way. Most people quit diets, feeling like a failure. But that is because most diets involve deprivation rather than moderation.

We need to stop feeling bad for enjoying food and enjoying life. Instead of taking away something that brings you happiness, focus on eating the food you enjoy in moderation. Deprivation leads to bitterness.

Now, can someone please pass me the pizza?

DECIDE AND DECLARE

- I get my value and worth from God—not people.
- I choose to enjoy my relationship with God; my relationship with myself; my relationship with others; my relationship with my body, with food and with money.
- I receive freedom from unhealthy relationships.
- I speak freedom over myself—freedom from co-dependency on anyone or anything.

- ◈ I am free from the cycle of shame, blame, finger-pointing and accusation toward myself or anyone else.
- ◈ I am persuaded of God's love and approval toward me.

Now Pray This with Me

Father, You created me to have and enjoy life. So today I choose to stop feeling bad and start enjoying life. Help me break free from the cycle of shame, blame and finger-pointing at myself or others. Thank You for giving me the power to stop living for crowd approval or people praise. Through You I reject shaming my body or anyone else's and instead I glorify you in my body as Your temple. And I'm persuaded and convinced of Your unconditional love and approval toward me. In Jesus' name I pray, Amen.

15

You Are More

Turning Your Pain into Purpose

In all these things we are more than conquerors through
Him who loved us.

Romans 8:37 MEV

S ong lyrics can capture the cries and mysteries of our souls. There
is one song in particular that really grabbed me when I first
heard it. Perhaps it will grab you as well. It is called "You Are
More," by a band called Tenth Avenue North.

There's a girl in the corner
With tear stains on her eyes
From the places she's wandered
And the shame she can't hide.
She says, how did I get here?
I'm not who I once was.
And I'm crippled by the fear
That I've fallen too far to love.

I wonder how many of us have been sitting alone with tears in our
eyes, filled with regret, shame, fear, anger, jealousy or any one of the
other soul thieves I have talked about in this book.

But then we miraculously allow ourselves to accept a gift, a reminder that we are loved by God, that we are His. It is as if we are allowed to reconnect with our Maker. So as the lyrics continue:

> But don't you know who you are,
> What's been done for you?
> Yeah, don't you know who you are?

And then these are the words that really drew me in:

> You are more than the choices that you've made,
> You are more than the sum of your past mistakes,
> You are more than the problems you create,
> You've been remade.

Yes! In His love and grace, God has remade you. He has washed you clean of all of your sins—the errors, missteps, resentments and all the wrong thinking that led to unhappiness. He promises that no shame, no mistake can define or limit the beautiful life He has reserved for you. And I am writing to remind you that you are so much more than the sum of your past mistakes, brokenness and heartaches. As the song finishes:

> 'Cause this is not about what you've done,
> But what's been done for you.
> This is not about where you've been,
> But where your brokenness brings you to
> This is not about what you feel,
> But what He felt to forgive you,
> And what He felt to make you loved.[1]

Even when we feel broken, we can be healed and find our way.
Socrates said: know yourself.
Sun Tzu said: know yourself.

226

Your inner self says: know yourself.

All because God is telling you: know yourself.

When you get hold of who you are and what you are living for:

It heals you.

It frees you.

It strengthens you.

It powers you through your pain.

But it starts with believing this:

You are more.

You are *more* than your pain.

You are *more* than your past.

You are *more* than your problems.

You are not defined by your imperfections. You are not average. You are not stuck. You are not limited. You are not bad. Yes, we are all human, but we are also treasured by God and remade in His image.

So you are more than even you think you are.

But so often in life, we feel less than, reminded of or reminding ourselves of what we cannot do, of what we are held back by. We are not good enough or smart enough or attractive enough or talented enough. Just not enough, period, right?

Maybe we feel we are the wrong color or age or height or weight, the wrong type to achieve our dreams. Auditioning actors are told no a thousand times, so much that rejection becomes meaningless. So what? Try anyway. Sometimes they land the role of a lifetime, and that changes everything.

Denzel Washington has spoken about his very first audition. He was told no. But he knew he could act. He knew God was with him. He knew who he was. So can you!

Consider this powerful verse from Scripture: "It's in Christ that we find out who we are and what we are living for. Long before we first heard of Christ and got our hopes up, he had his eye on us, had designs on us for glorious living, part of the overall purpose he is working out in everything and everyone" (Ephesians 1:11–12 MSG).

Have you ever looked at an informational map at a mall? I have, many times. You are trying to find the fastest way to your destination. And what's the first thing you look for when you look at the map? For me, it is the YOU ARE HERE marker. Because until you know where you are, you cannot get where you are going.

So even when we feel lost, we need a map in our heads to continually remind us, "You are here!" Where? In Christ. Only in Him do we find out who we are and what we are living for. That is the compass that shows us that we are called, anointed, and appointed for something more than we imagined. This knowledge will lead you to better decisions, decisions that will in turn lead you to your God-given destiny.

You Were Made for More

> A man without a vision is a man without a future. A man without a future will always return to his past.
>
> P. K. Bernard

If you do not have a vision, you will often return to your past, whether it involves addiction, crime, an unhealthy relationship or something else.

But the first thing God does in people's lives when they encounter Him is give them a vision—a sense of purpose, a way to make a difference, a way to make life matter. When we do not feel as if we "count," we suffer. We are built to endure, but when we do not have the "why" for our lives, we lose hope. That has a mental and emotional impact on us.

I believe that having a vision and purpose for our lives is powerful. I believe:

◆ Purpose breaks the power of boredom.
◆ Purpose breaks the power of distraction.

◈ Purpose breaks the power of depression.

◈ Purpose breaks the power of pain and limitations.

◈ Purpose breaks the power of fear.

◈ Purpose breaks the power of the past.

◈ Purpose breaks the power of addiction.

God has designed and handpicked you for a purpose, a reason: "Before I formed you in the womb I knew you, and before you were born I consecrated you; I have appointed you" (Jeremiah 1:5).

I want to give you a quick shortcut to discovering your purpose. It is something I have talked about for years and wrote an entire chapter about in my book *The Power to Change Today*.

It is simply this: Your calling is found in your conquering.

In other words, whatever you have conquered in your life is usually what leads you to the purpose you have been created for.

And as you conquer what is right in front of you, it usually takes you to the next step in your life's purpose and journey. *The thing right in front of us holds the key to what is well beyond us right now.* It is often the thing right in front of us that we are skipping over to "find ourselves."

You can change that mindset today and catapult yourself to the next chapter, next level, and next season of your life.

For example, if you have a conflict with someone, conquer it. I do not mean conquer or clobber the person. 😄 But be proactive in resolving the matter. Because the resolution holds the key to the next door you are supposed to go through.

> Your calling is found in your conquering.

Or maybe you want to start a business. But what kind of employee have you been in someone else's business? Do you see? Conquer your current position—master it—and you will be promoted. Conquer a few promotions, and you are well on your way to starting your own business. It starts with thinking like an owner, then acting like one.

Powering Past Pain

We all know what it is like to hurt. To be hurt by others—the pain of being misunderstood, walked on, taken advantage of, even abused; the pain of betrayal, failure, disappointment, feeling useless and underappreciated.

What can we do about it? Well, I am glad you asked: "Yea, they turned back and tempted God, and limited the Holy One of Israel" (Psalm 78:41 KJV). Notice the word *limited* in this verse.

Now compare it to a different translation: "Again and again they tempted God, and pained the Holy One of Israel." Here, the word *pained* is used instead of *limited*. Therefore, they are interchangeable.

In other words, our pain is what limits us, and what limits us causes pain. So guess what? It is time to break out of our limitations. And break out of our pain.

In the original Hebrew, the word is *tavah*, which means "to pain" or "to wound." It can also mean "to mark out."

Whatever is hurting you right now is not going to limit you. It is not going to mark you out. It has knocked you down, but it will not knock you out.

We can probably learn a few things about feeling pain, and feeling limited, by a guy named Pain. Yes, there is a man in the Bible whose mother named him Pain.

Have you ever been called a pain in the a#@ by someone? That is a good sign it is going to be a bad day! But at least your mother did not name you Pain: "Now Jabez was more honorable than his brothers, and his mother called his name Jabez, saying, 'Because I bore him in pain'" (1 Chronicles 4:9 NKJV).

Jabez was more honorable than his brothers, but his mother still called him Jabez because that word in Hebrew means "pain." It seems strange. But let's break it down: Jabez brought pain to his mother during his birth—pain so excruciating that she wanted him to remember what he put her through for the rest of his life. Actually, that is not strange at all! All our mothers remind us of that in one way or another, right? Haha.

Notice that despite the pain Jabez caused his mother, he was more honorable than his brothers. To be more honorable means to live in a way that makes you bigger than the disadvantages you have experienced.

Jabez rose above his natural limitations. He went beyond his pain. He rose above his human capacity. His life counted for something greater than the ground or family curse he came from.

All his brothers were born from the same parents, but Jabez made some choices that distinguished him from his brothers. These choices are laid out for us in the very next verse: "And Jabez called on the God of Israel saying, 'Oh, that You would bless me indeed, and enlarge my territory, that Your hand would be with me, and that You would keep me from evil, that I may not cause pain!' So God granted him what he requested" (1 Chronicles 4:10 NKJV).

This verse, known as the Prayer of Jabez, gives us several strategic keys to moving our lives beyond pain and limitation.

1. The first one is this: Jabez did something about his situation.

He went to God. When you are hurting, when you feel limited, when you feel life has closed in on you, you can always go to God. It seems so simple because . . . well, it is!

You have every right to be set free, because Jesus bore your pain. This is part of the great exchange that God offers us. Jesus became sin so that we could become righteous. He became cursed so that we could be blessed. He took our pain so that we could have healing, freedom and a life not bound or limited by the past.

Have you ever said this: "This darn warning light keeps going on in my car. It's so annoying." No, it is not annoying—it is a blessing! It is a signal (i.e., a *sign*-al) telling you that there is a problem you have to take the time to fix. Jabez interpreted his pain as a signal rather than a prison sentence. It was a signal to do something about it.

2. Pain is a signal to pray.

We should not suppress it or ignore it. It is a signal to go to God. A signal to shake off whatever leech is clinging to you, sucking the life and enjoyment out of your existence. Something hurting you? Go to God.

3. Jabez refused to be defined by his pain.

He refused to be confined by what his mother named him. She called him Pain, but he rejected that label. He believed he was more. And so should you.

People will try to define us. Our mistakes will try to define us. And the enemy will try to confine us. We must refuse to accept the labels others try to put on us. Labels = limits. And we serve a God who is limitless. So let's be defined by what God calls us and refuse to be defined by anything or anyone else.

Are you ready to refuse to accept the pain and limitations of your life? Are you ready for more? Then it is time to ask for more.

4. Jabez went big.

He went bold. He went beyond his upbringing. He prayed: "Bless me indeed, and enlarge my territory." Notice that he was not going to just settle for healing. He wanted something greater—a blessing, which confers so much more than healing. It offers everything Jesus paid for with His precious blood. Being blessed means to be empowered to succeed in every area of life.

You don't think that is possible? Here is an example: "Now Abraham was old, advanced in age; and the LORD had blessed Abraham in every way" (Genesis 24:1). *And what does Abraham's blessing have to do with me?* you might ask. Again, I am glad you did. The answer is that whatever God did in Abraham's life, He promises to do in your life, too: "And if you belong to Christ, then you are Abraham's seed, heirs according to the promise" (Galatians 3:29 csb).

You see, because you are in Christ, God promises that He will do for you what He did for Abraham—and for Jabez, for that matter. So go bold. Go big. Go beyond. Ask bigger. Ask for the blessing.

5. He refused to settle.

He was not going to let his pain stop him from growing, expanding, taking more ground. You cannot let it stop you, either. Jabez asked God to enlarge his territory.

We really would love to receive what God has promised, but something inside us often says, *You don't deserve it. You are not good enough. You haven't prayed long enough. You haven't done this, but you've done a lot of that.*

In other words, our feelings of unworthiness cause us to object to or reject the favors God is extending to us. As I said on page 107, instead of holding our arms out and our palms up, showing that we are ready to receive His blessings, we push the blessings away. We do this because we do not feel worthy.

What delivers us from shame and unworthiness? Jesus does. He gives us His righteousness and His royalty. And remember that royalty destroys inferiority and renews our minds so that we feel worthy of the best God has to offer.

Let's Change It Today

Isn't it time to take more ground in your life? To live with greater purpose? To walk in the favor of answered prayers? To realize your dreams? To live the God-given life you were born for?

My friend, in order to enlarge your territory, you have to get down to earth and realize that you are in this life to have a positive impact on other people for Jesus' sake.

What is the new ground or territory you need to take today? Is it in the realm of your finances? Your family? Your health? Do you need healing or freedom from an addiction? Never let the devil shame you into thinking you are asking for too much.

Refuse to settle. Be uncomfortable with staying where you are. Ask God to give you new territory—a new business, a new career, a new healthy relationship. It is time to capture new ground.

It is time to expand and grow. Refuse to be confined in a corner of life. Pray that right now: "O God, enlarge my territory. Give me new ground; expand my borders. Increase my impact in this world."

Jesus did not come to earth to be the greatest teacher of all time, although He most certainly was that. He also came to save us, then elevate us to our true worth and purpose—to proclaim our value and and to prove our true worth.

Jabez knew that he needed a hand.

Jabez prayed that God's hand would be with him. He knew that healing flows from God's hand; that strength, help and favor flow from His hand. The hand of God represents several things in the Bible:

- ◈ His hand represents acceptance and approval.
- ◈ His hand represents protection and power.
- ◈ His hand represents anointing and authority.
- ◈ His hand represents provision and supply.
- ◈ His hand represents direction and guidance.

Our own hands are not enough to heal ourselves, to enlarge ourselves or to open doors that we cannot close. But His hands are more than enough.

This means that you are not stuck. You are not limited to what mere human hands can do. The hand of divinity and authority is upon you. The hand of favor and blessing is upon you. The hand of protection and provision is upon you.

Whatever you see Jesus do with His hands in the Bible is what He wants to do in your life. He made us. He saved us. He raised us. He holds us. He heals us. He raises us. He comforts us. He molds us. He blesses us. And with His hands, He leads us, pulling us forward. With His hands, He also applauds us and encourages us, just as a parent or coach would. But so much more.

Expect God's hand to guide and provide today.

Jabez knew that he was made for more.

Jabez knew he was made for more than what his name signified. When he prayed "Keep me from evil, that I may not cause pain," he wanted God to use him to bring healing.

Notice that Jabez equated evil with causing pain. Every one of us has a choice of the kind of life we want to live. What is our choice? What are we bringing to other people's lives? Are we bringing them pain? Or are we bringing them healing?

If we want our lives to count for more, then we need to decide to bring something to others that lifts their lives, something that heals them in some way. When some people come into our lives, it hurts! When others come into our lives, it heals. Let's be healers.

To review: What made Jabez more honorable than his brothers?

- He did something about his situation—He went to God.
- He interpreted pain as a signal to pray.
- He refused to be defined by his pain.
- He went big. He went bold. He went for the blessing.
- He refused to settle.
- He expected God's hand to guide and provide.
- He knew he was made for more.

And I will add this:

Jabez had to give himself permission to be distinguished from the people he grew up with.

It does not mean he thought he was better. But he was not afraid to stand out in the crowd. So give yourself permission to be everything God created you to be, no matter what anyone thinks or says about you.

Will you be bold with me and decide to live a life that brings healing, not pain?

I am asking you, inviting you, even daring you to go where you have never gone before. You cannot ask too much of God. He said He would give you abundantly above what you can ask for, blessings that are infinitely beyond your wildest dreams. Let's dare to be bold in our prayers. Our God is not limited. Let's be bold in believing that our past, our pain and our problems will never again define us and that they will no longer confine us.

> You cannot ask too much of God.

Let's treat our pain as a signal to think big, ask big, and dream big. Let's choose to let our pain make us better, not bitter. Let's refuse to become the person that pain says we are. Let's accept only who God says we are.

And let's choose to take more ground and receive all the blessings that Jesus paid so dearly for us to share. Expect God to grant your request, just as He granted Jabez's. And then thank Him.

A final thought on having a vision for your life. . . . Close your eyes and imagine for a moment the kind of person you admire most. Now decide to become that person. And then give that person as a gift to the world. Because living in the service of others is the only life truly worth living.

DECIDE AND DECLARE

◈ I receive healing from my pain.
◈ I am breaking free of my limitations.
◈ I choose to bring healing, not pain.
◈ I accept God's help and His hand of power in my life.

Now Pray This with Me

Heavenly Father, though I have had pain and limitations, I am asking You to bless me indeed. I hope to receive healing from my pain, but I also expect to break free of my limitations. I am asking big today, Lord. Enlarge my territory, give me new ground, maximize my impact, enlarge my life. You are not limited, so I will stop thinking limited.

Thank You for keeping Your hand upon me. I expect Your help and Your hand of protection, provision and power. I am asking you to use my life to bring blessing and healing to other people as I step into this next chapter and season of my life's purpose, in Jesus' name.

16

Your Story Doesn't End Here

There has never been the slightest doubt in my mind that the God who started this great work in you would keep at it and bring it to a flourishing finish on the very day Christ Jesus appears.

Philippians 1:6 MSG

For each of us, the days ahead will include mistakes, wrong turns, conflicting emotions, controversial decisions and uncertainty. And that's okay.

Because God's purpose for you is not limited by your mistakes or wrong turns. God is the ultimate GPS navigational system. If you miss a turn on the path of life, God knows how to recalculate the next route. This is a powerful truth that will bring you much peace and calm, no matter what is happening inside or around you.

Finding God's will and His peace in your life is not some wild-goose chase. He is the one who found you. You have not tied His hands behind His back with your crazy days, months or years. You have not failed, no matter how many times you think you have failed. How do I know that?

Because your life is a story. And God is the author and finisher of the story of your life (see Hebrews 12:2).

Life is not meant to be a snapshot or frozen-in-time tableau or selfie that confines and defines you. Life is meant to be lived as an unfolding story. "This is the story of how it all started, of Heaven and Earth when they were created" (Genesis 2:4 MSG). A great story is how life began. And a great story is how it will end.

> God is the author and finisher of the story of your life.

This book, *Soul Cure*, starts with a story. It is filled with stories. Some are from the Bible. Some are from my life's journey. Some are from life in general.

The Bible itself is a story. It is a motion picture. But we have read it wrong. We have been taught it wrong. Therefore we set ourselves up for disappointment, because we are expecting it to be so linear—written and read in a straight line. But the Bible isn't meant to be experienced like that. Because life isn't experienced like that.

Think about it: We do not see anyone's *entire* life in the Bible. We see the highlights—the victories and defeats. But we do not see all that came before, after or in between.

Most people read the Bible linearly, as sentences and paragraphs and black and white rules. But the Bible is not a straight line. Neither is life. It is a collection of real-life stories. And the stories are what we remember most.

◈ Adam and Eve
◈ David and Goliath
◈ Samson and Delilah
◈ Moses parting the Red Sea
◈ Noah and the flood
◈ Abraham and Sarah

- Joseph and his coat of many colors
- Joseph thrown into a pit and sold into slavery
- Jesus and the man born blind
- Jesus and Lazarus
- Jesus and the woman at the well
- Jesus and the lame man at the pool of Bethesda
- Jesus and the woman caught in adultery
- Paul and Silas in prison

The list goes on and on. There was the story of the pearl of great price. The story of the ten virgins, the ten lepers, the ten coins. The story of a short guy climbing up a tree to see Jesus. The story of the best wine ever served in human history. The story of seeds and four types of soil. The story of the good Samaritan. The story of the friend at midnight who had no shame. The story of a lost son, a bitter brother and a loving father who all got a second chance. The story of the widow who would not take no for an answer. The story of the woman who had been bleeding for twelve years and was healed when she touched the hem of His garment. According to Scripture, Jesus was one to "tell stories" (Matthew 13:34 MSG).

We remember the Bible's stories just as we remember our life's stories. Our memories are not made up of words or sentences. They are made up of images, plotlines, events that have shaped our lives in one way or another.

One of the great frustrations of human existence occurs because we have somehow bought the notion that life is supposed to be lived in a straight line.

We are born. We go to school. We go to college. We meet our soulmates. We have children. We have grandchildren. We die. The end.

Except . . . it isn't. It is never quite like that, is it?

We have a plan, then life takes a sharp turn. As the saying goes, if you want to make God laugh, tell Him your plans. We thought we were going straight, then we are falling off a cliff. Or we are divorced. Or a child dies. Or we lose a job, a business or our life savings. Well, guess what? Your story doesn't end there!

You see, I believe that emotions play the biggest role in our life stories. Our emotions are not linear. They are not straight lines. They are e-*motions*. They are constantly moving, constantly fluctuating.

If we would see our lives in motion, we would see that they do not move in a straight line, either. They are all over the place. Ever felt like that? All over the place? I have felt like that a lot.

But God is the author *and* the finisher. He is not going to let your life end on a sour note or a bad chapter. He will not let it end with a bad year, bad marriage or bad decade. No. God is causing all things to work together for good for you.

When we think that life is going to end horribly, we lose hope and peace. Maybe your life is in the middle of a horror story right now. But your story doesn't end there. If your life is not great yet, it is not finished yet. God is not finished yet. He is just getting started.

It is amazing to me that young people these days feel like if they hit 25 or 30 years old and do not have a spouse, two and a half kids, and a two-and-a-half-car garage, then somehow life is over. But it ain't even close! It is just getting started.

Think of some of the well-known miracle stories that did not start out so great.

Legend has it that Walt Disney was turned down 302 times before finally getting financing for his dream of creating Walt Disney World.[1] It has also been said that Colonel Sanders, founder of Kentucky Fried Chicken, was rejected 1,009 times before finding a taker for his chicken recipe.[2] He was 65 years old. Talk about "finger-lickin' good."

The same goes for you. You might be in chapter 1, chapter 100 or chapter 1008 of your story, but it doesn't end there.

When Steve Jobs was only twenty years old, he started Apple in his parents' garage, and within a decade the company blossomed into a $2 billion empire. When Jobs was thirty, however, Apple's board of directors decided to take the business in a different direction, and Jobs was fired from the company he created. Jobs found himself unemployed, but he treated it as a blessing rather than a curse. You see? His story did not end there. He later said that getting fired from Apple was the best thing that ever happened to him because it allowed him to think more creatively and reexperience the joys of starting a company.[3]

Jobs went on to found NeXT, a software company, and Pixar, the company that produces animated movies such as *Finding Nemo*. NeXT was subsequently purchased by Apple. Not only did Jobs go back to his former company, but he also helped launch Apple's resurgence and long-lasting tradition of innovation. Jobs claimed that his career success and his strong relationship with his family were both results of his termination from Apple. Wow!

What does all this have to do with soul power and soul cure?

Glad you asked.

The answer: everything.

You see, our minds play tricks on us if we are not careful.

They will tell us there is no hope. Which leads to depression.

They will tell us that there is nobody. Which leads to loneliness.

They will tell us that there is no coming back from failure. Which leads to shame.

Our emotions follow our belief systems. And when you look at your life as a snapshot, you may feel depressed, lonely or ashamed. When you look at your life linearly, you may treat every wrong turn and winding road as a crisis. If life is not cut-and-dried or black-and-white, it can create a bit—or a boatload—of anxiety.

Let's say you take a really good selfie, in which you are smiling and on top of the world, but guess what? It took you 45 tries to get one that made you look good. So that is kind of discouraging, too. Haha.

But your life does not consist of a selfie, good or bad. Your life consists of a beautiful, turbulent, fascinating collection of seasons, chapters and episodes that culminate in a glorious ending that you have not arrived at yet.

242

And when you grab hold of this idea, it affects your emotions in a positive way. It gives you hope of turning to a better page. A better chapter. A better ending.

You're Headed for a Happy Ending

> If you want a happy ending, that depends, of course, on where you stop your story.
>
> Orson Welles

Your happy ending begins when you realize that it does not end where it is right now.

This is why we love movies so much. All movies tell a story. They are our stories, distilled into two- or three-hour segments.

And many of them have the word *story* in their titles: *Toy Story. L.A. Story. West Side Story. The Philadelphia Story. Police Story. Ghost Story. Rogue One: A Star Wars Story. Love Story.*

Think about some of the greatest authors of all time: William Shakespeare. Oscar Wilde. Mark Twain. Victor Hugo. Frederick Douglass. Maya Angelou. C. S. Lewis. Think about the stories they created. The drama. The intrigue. The twists and turns. Some chapters are cliff-hangers. Some chapters tie things together. Some chapters are, well, pretty depressing.

I have got good news for you. No matter what chapter your life is in, no matter how bad it may seem, no matter what you might be facing at this very moment, your story does not end there.

If these great authors can leave the reader hanging on every word, leave the reader eager to turn to the next page, the next paragraph, the next chapter, just think how good God is at it.

In Hebrews 12:2, Paul describes Jesus as the author and finisher of our faith. But He is not just any author. He is the greatest author. As well as the greatest finisher. He does not just start the story of your life. He finishes it.

You and I are living in what I call the "in-between." God started your life, and He knows how it is going to end. But in between is where the drama lies. It's where the mysteries unfold. Your "in-between" might not feel very good, but your story doesn't end there.

Remember the story of Lazarus, the brother of Mary and Martha? While he was sick, his sisters reached out to Jesus and ask Him to heal Lazarus. When Jesus hears about it, He says, "This sickness will not end in death" (John 11:4 HCSB).

It will not end in death? But it did end in death. Didn't it?

No. Lazarus's story *included* death, but did not *end* in death.

In other words, yes, Lazarus did die of the sickness, but his story did not end there. After he was dead for four days, Jesus raised him back to life when He said, "Lazarus, come forth!" (John 11:43 NKJV).

> **Your story doesn't end there.**

What's the point? The point is, well, sometimes things get worse before they get better. But your story doesn't end there. Things may have gotten worse for you financially, or physically, or emotionally, but your story doesn't end there.

Something I have learned in my own life is that it is never too late for God, no matter how bad the situation is. God's timing is not my timing. But I will take His any day. Because "He has made every thing beautiful in his time" (Ecclesiastes 3:11 JUB). If it is not beautiful yet, it is not time yet.

Your life is a motion picture. It is moving. It is changing. It is heading toward an amazing, unfolding, beautiful crescendo. "Your eyes saw my substance, being yet unformed. And in Your book they all were written, the days fashioned for me, when as yet there were none of them" (Psalm 139:16 NKJV).

You see? Your story is written by God. It does not mean that everything that happens in your life was predetermined. It just means that no matter what happens in your life, God knows how to turn the bad into something good. He knows how to take the weapons trained on you and turn them around.

As I said earlier, what the enemy sends to defeat you, God bends to complete you.

It's All about Perspective

When you change the way you see things, it changes how you feel about things. You do not always need things to *be* different. You just need to *see* different.

Someone once said, "We all are faced with a series of great opportunities brilliantly disguised as impossible situations."[4] But it is amazing that two people can see the same thing and have two completely different reactions.

I once heard a story about two shoe salesmen who were dispatched to the same remote village in Africa around one hundred years ago. One sent a telegram to his boss that said, "Get me home. Nobody here wears shoes." The other salesman's telegram said, "Send me all the shoes you can! Nobody here wears shoes!"

The facts were the same. But the perspective changed everything.

Consider a story that Thomas Wheeler, the retired CEO of Massachusetts Mutual Life Insurance, tells about himself.

[He] and his wife were driving along an interstate highway when he noticed that their car was low on gas. Wheeler got off the highway at the next exit and soon found a rundown gas station with just one pump. He asked the lone attendant to fill the tank and check the oil, then went for a little walk around the station to stretch his legs.

As he was returning to the car, he noticed that the attendant and his wife were engaged in an animated conversation. The conversation stopped when he paid the attendant. But after Wheeler got back into the car, he saw the attendant wave at his wife and heard him say, "It was great talking to you."

As they drove out of the station, Wheeler asked his wife if she knew the man. She readily admitted she did. They had gone to high school together and had dated steadily for around a year.

"Boy, were you lucky that I came along," bragged Wheeler. "If you had married him, you'd be the wife of a gas station attendant instead of the wife of a chief executive officer."

"My dear," replied his wife, "if I had married him, he'd be the chief executive officer and you'd be the gas station attendant."[5]

Wheeler's wife sure had the right perspective.

Here is another example: When David's brothers saw Goliath, they thought, *He's so big, we can never kill him.* When David saw Goliath, he thought, *He's so big, I can't miss him!*

They all saw the same Goliath. They just saw him differently. Maybe because they saw themselves differently. The way we see other people is almost always a reflection of the way we see ourselves.

If David was so confident that he could not miss, why did he carry "five smooth stones" (1 Samuel 17:40)? Because Goliath had four brothers (see 2 Samuel 21:15–22), and David was ready for all of 'em.

You cannot miss. God is with you. You have His Word. You have His promises. You have a covenant with Him.

Where Does My Story End?

Consider the story of King David's life. He was the forgotten youngest son of Jesse, brother of seven warriors, none of whom thought he could fight. But his story didn't end there.

When he was left alone with a herd of helpless sheep instead of being sent into battle, he could have become bitter and angry at his father and brothers, but his story didn't end there.

When the sheep were threatened by a lion, he could have been killed, but his story didn't end there.

When he was attacked by a bear, he could have been the bear's lunch. But his story didn't end there.

When his brothers ran from Goliath, he could have run, too, but his story didn't end there.

Goliath could have crushed him with his bare hands, but his story didn't end there. (You starting to see a pattern here?)

When King Saul threw a spear at him, he could have been killed, but his story didn't end there.

When he committed adultery with Bathsheba, his story didn't end there.

When he allowed Uriah, Bathsheba's husband, to be killed in battle, his story didn't end there.

He could have been sentenced to life in prison for murder, but his story didn't end there.

He could have been overtaken with depression at the death of his son, but his story didn't end there.

He could have been consumed with rage and bitterness after his son Absalom betrayed him, stealing the hearts of his men, but his story didn't end there.

"God removed Saul and replaced him with David, a man about whom God said, 'I have found David son of Jesse, a man after my own heart. He will do everything I want him to do'" (Acts 13:22 NLT).

"For David, after he had served God's purpose in his own generation, fell asleep, and was buried among his fathers and underwent decay" (Acts 13:36).

Isn't it amazing? Even though David failed many times and made many bad, life-altering decisions, still, God said, when reflecting on David's life, "He did everything I wanted him to do." His story didn't end with his failures. The last word about David? He served the purpose of God, then fell asleep. He died, having fulfilled God's will, closing the last chapter of his story. And that can be your story, too.

Like David, we all face rejection. We all face a giant, as David did, but God is on our side. We all face a huge mistake we made—and maybe make a bigger one to cover it up, as David did. But God is on our side. We are reminded in the great psalm 51, verse 12, that God will restore to us the joy of His salvation, even after our darkest days . . . because our story doesn't end there.

Your story is unfolding. It may not feel like a happy ending, but *it has not ended*. There are many more chapters yet to be read. They are written by God. But not yet revealed.

Your life is a story. So get your popcorn ready!

You cannot always control the highs and lows in life. Those moments are not constant. They change. But there is one constant in your life: You can always give glory to God. You can glorify Him in good times. And bad. Clear times and foggy.

When you are on the top of the mountain, give Him glory, because it is He who got you there. At the bottom of the valley, give Him glory, because it is He who is with you there.

These overarching beliefs have to pervade your thinking:

- God's goodness is chasing you, following you all the days of your life. You cannot outrun the goodness of God.
- No matter what the enemy sends to defeat you, God bends to complete you.
- You possess the victory in every situation in life. It's just a matter of time.
- You are more than a conqueror through Christ.
- Jesus is the author and finisher of your faith.

Jesus' own life provides numerous examples of setbacks and obstacles. For example, He was deeply troubled in the Garden of Gethsemane, but His story didn't end there.

He was whipped and beaten, but His story didn't end there.

He was crucified. Died. And buried. But His story didn't end there.

He was stripped of all human dignity, suffering for us on the cross. But His story didn't end there.

Jesus died on a Friday, but His story didn't end there.

Nothing happened on Saturday. But His story didn't end there.

Look at your life right at this moment.

Are you in Friday? At Gethsemane? At the trial? At the scourging? Feeling lonely?

Are you in Saturday? In uncertainty and darkness? Perplexed and confused? Depressed? Anxious? Stressed?

Or are you in Sunday? In the resurrection chapter of life?

If it is Friday, your story doesn't end there. If it is Saturday, your story doesn't end there.

Sunday is comin'!

If you are depressed right now, your story doesn't end there.

If you are discouraged right now, your story doesn't end there.

I was high on drugs every day of my young life, but my story didn't end there.

I was depressed and suicidal. But my story didn't end there.

Suddenly I was saved and became an evangelist, but my story didn't end there.

I became a husband and father, but my story didn't end there.

I became a pastor and leader, but my story didn't end there.

No matter where you think you are right now, your story doesn't end there.

When you get discouraged, read and reread this amazing verse of Scripture:

> Keep your eyes on Jesus, who both began and finished this race we're in. Study how he did it. Because he never lost sight of where he was headed— that exhilarating finish in and with God—he could put up with anything along the way: Cross, shame, whatever. And now he's there, in the place of honor, right alongside God. When you find yourselves flagging in your faith, go over that story again, item by item, that long litany of hostility he plowed through. That will shoot adrenaline into your souls!
>
> Hebrews 12:2–3 MSG

Who is ready for some holy adrenaline shots in the bloodstream of your soul?

So how do you enjoy your story, and honor the author of it, when you are going through a bad chapter in life?

1. Believe your life is a love story.

Your life is not just any old story. It is a love story between you and God, and you are the star. The author created *you* especially for this role: "Your love, GOD, is my song, and I'll sing it! I'm forever telling everyone how faithful you are. I'll never quit telling the story of your love" (Psalm 89:1 MSG).

2. Believe the story will end with love.

Your story is going to end with God's love, protection, comfort, power and goodness.

> The people of Israel are going to live a long time stripped of security and protection, without religion and comfort, godless and prayerless. But in time they'll come back, these Israelites, come back looking for their GOD and their David-King. They'll come back chastened to reverence before GOD and his good gifts, ready for the End of the story of his love.
>
> Hosea 3:4 MSG

3. Shift your perspective.

Look at your current life situation as just a chapter in a book, a page in a script, a scene in a film. Great stories are made of drama, mystery and challenges. That is what keeps your attention and keeps you interested. What if we looked at our lives that way? What if we knew there was going to be a happy ending? How anxious do you think we would be? How depressed do you think we would be? How angry could we be if we really knew that God is going to sort it all out and bring us through to the end?

Our perspective affects our emotions and our souls. King David said, "I would have despaired unless I had believed that I would see the goodness of the LORD in the land of the living" (Psalm 27:13 NASB1995). Do you see the effect that perspective has on your emotions? Despair is one of the worst feelings. And yet it is swallowed up when you believe you are going to experience God's goodness.

God does not cause all things. But He "causes all things to work together for good" (Romans 8:28).

4. Look for the good.

Look forward with expectation. Expect good to come. Look for the goodness of God in the silver lining of every cloud. "There has never been the slightest doubt in my mind that the God who started this great work in you would keep at it and bring it to a flourishing finish on the very day Christ Jesus appears" (Philippians 1:6 MSG). Give yourself permission to enjoy your life.

No matter what's going on in your life in this moment, your story doesn't end there.

5. Trust God.

We don't want you in the dark, friends, about how hard it was when all this came down on us in Asia province. It was so bad we didn't think we were going to make it. We felt like we'd been sent to death row, that it was all over for us. As it turned out, it was the best thing that could have happened. Instead of trusting in our own strength or wits to get out of it, we were forced to trust God totally—*not a bad idea since he's the God who raises the dead!* And he did it, rescued us from certain doom. And he'll do it again, rescuing us as many times as we need rescuing. You and your prayers are part of the rescue operation—I don't want you in the dark about that either. I can see your faces even now, lifted in praise for God's deliverance of us, a rescue in which your prayers played such a crucial part.

2 Corinthians 1:8 MSG, emphasis added

I love the sentence "We were forced to trust God totally—not a bad idea since he's the God who raises the dead!" Wow! Believe that today. And everything is gonna be all right.

6. Tell your story.

"As Jesus was getting into the boat, the demon-delivered man begged to go along, but he wouldn't let him. Jesus said, 'Go home to your own people. Tell them your story—what the Master did, how he had mercy on you'" (Mark 5:19 MSG).

"Then you can tell the next generation detail by detail the story of God, our God forever, who guides us till the end of time" (Psalm 48:13 MSG).

7. *Choose to live by faith, not fear.*

Do you see what this means—all these pioneers who blazed the way, all these veterans cheering us on? It means we'd better get on with it. Strip down, start running—and never quit! No extra spiritual fat, no parasitic sins. Keep your eyes on Jesus, who both began and finished this race we're in. Study how he did it. Because he never lost sight of where he was headed—that exhilarating finish in and with God—he could put up with anything along the way: Cross, shame, whatever. And now he's there, in the place of honor, right alongside God. When you find yourselves flagging in your faith, go over that story again, item by item, that long litany of hostility he plowed through. That will shoot adrenaline into your souls!

Hebrews 12:1–3 MSG

Well, there is the adrenaline. I hope you feel it pumping through your veins right now. You can put up with anything along the way when you know that your story will not end in the midst of a chapter filled with brokenness, pain and tears. Fix your eyes on Jesus. He loves you. He has called you. He chose you. And He will finish what He started in you.

Of that you can be sure. And when you believe that, everything is gonna be all right.

DECIDE AND DECLARE

- ❖ My life is a story. And it doesn't end here.
- ❖ My life doesn't end in failure, heartbreak, sadness or fear.
- ❖ If my life isn't great yet, it simply means my story isn't over yet.

- No matter how I've been treated, my story doesn't end there.
- No matter how I've failed, my story doesn't end there.
- No matter how much trouble I've seen, my story doesn't end there.
- Whatever enemy of my life or soul has been chasing me, my story doesn't end there.
- I will see the goodness of God in my life today because my story doesn't end here!

Now Pray This with Me

Heavenly Father, I thank You that my story is continuing to get better and better. No matter how many bad chapters I've lived, my best days are my next days. Your goodness is overtaking the bad in my life. Your goodness is overtaking my enemies. Your goodness is following me, chasing me and overtaking me. And I thank You that all things are working together for my good. No matter what is going on in my life, my story doesn't end here. You said my life will be like the light of dawn, getting brighter and brighter until the full day, in Jesus' name, Amen.

APPENDIX

Deciding and Declaring God's Love

I will greet this day with God's love in my heart! It is the secret to fulfillment. It is the source of all healing inside and out. It brings success, no matter what life throws at me. It calms every storm. It silences every enemy. It fills every empty part of my soul. It comforts me. When I face darkness, it brings light. When I'm overwhelmed, it inspires and encourages me. When I'm distressed, it reminds me of God's goodness. When I feel discouraged, it lifts my hands to the Lord and fills my mouth with song.

I will greet this day with God's love in my heart! When it feels like heaven is silent, God's love will remind me that He knows what I'm going through. He has a plan. And He will provide for my every need.

I will greet this day with God's love in my heart! Love will lead me. Love will direct me. Love will inspire me. Love will heal me. Love will fill me. Love will revive me.

I will greet this day with God's love in my heart! Love will deliver me from my enemies. It will protect me in times of danger. It will redirect the arrows of the wicked one. Because of God's love, all those who seek to hurt me will be stopped, for love makes my shield of faith strong.

I will greet this day with God's love in my heart! And I will love all whom I come in contact with today. I will love the weak and make them strong. I will love the inspired and be inspired by them. I will love the empty and help them be filled. I will love the filled, and they will overflow! I will love the broken, and they will be healed. I will confront everyone I meet with love. It will shine through my eyes, bring a smile to my lips, and sound out through my voice. It will bring peace. It will lower people's defenses and empower them to experience God's presence.

I will greet this day with God's love in my heart! Because He loves me, I will love myself. I will love others. And I will love life, no matter what I face. From this moment forward, fear and hate leave my body and my mind. Fear and hate leave my family and my home, in Jesus' name!

I will worship God this day with His love in my heart!

Notes

Introduction

1. "The World Health Report 2001: Mental Disorders Affect One in Four People," World Health Organization, September 28, 2001, https://www.who.int/news/item /28-09-2001-the-world-health-report-2001-mental-disorders-affect-one-in-four -people.

Chapter 1 "Someone Has Stolen Our Tent!"

1. Christian Nordqvist, "One Million People Commit Suicide Each Year—World Suicide Prevention Day, September 10, 2011," *Medical News Today*, September 11, 2011, https://www.medicalnewstoday.com/articles/234219.

2. Josh Hafner, "Surgeon General: 1 in 7 in USA Will Face Substance Addiction," *USA Today*, November 16, 2016, https://www.usatoday.com/story/news/nation-now /2016/11/17/surgeon-general-1-7-us-face-substance-addiction/93993474/.

3. "Statistics," National Coalition Against Domestic Violence, accessed October 18, 2021, https://ncadv.org/statistics.

4. "Eating Order Statistics," South Carolina Department of Mental Health, accessed October 18, 2021, https://www.state.sc.us/dmh/anorexia/statistics.htm.

5. "Suicide," National Institude of Mental Health, accessed October 18, 2021, https://www.nimh.nih.gov/health/statistics/suicide.

6. Harry Zhang, "Self Inflicted Injuries amond Children in the United States—Estimates from a Nationwide Emergency Department Sample," U.S. National Library of Medicine National Institutes of Health, July 18, 2013, https://www.ncbi.nlm.nih .gov/pmc/articles/PMC3715517/.

7. Blaise Pascal, *Human Happiness*, trans. A. J. Krailsheimer (New York: Penguin, 2008), 148.

Chapter 2 Feed Your Soul Beauty

1. Gregory Dickow, "The Beauty of Jesus: Remedy for a Discouraged Soul," September 25, 2020, https://gregorydickow.com/the-beauty-of-jesus/.

2. Dickow, "The Beauty of Jesus."

3. Dickow, "The Beauty of Jesus."

4. "988 Vladimir Adopts Christianity," Christian History Institute, accessed October 18, 2021, https://christianhistoryinstitute.org/magazine/article/vladimir-adopts -christianity.

5. "Altogether Lovely," words and music by Wendell P. Loveless ©1931, Ren. 1959 Hope Publishing Company, Carol Stream, IL 60188. All rights reserved. Used by permission.

Chapter 4 Get Swept Away

1. Salynn Boyles, "Romantic Love Affects Your Brain Like a Drug," WebMD, October 13, 2010, https://www.webmd.com/pain-management/news/20101013 /romantic-love-affects-your-brain-like-a-drug#2.

2. Abigail Fagan, "Touching Empathy," Psychology Today, March 1, 2020, https:// www.psychologytoday.com/us/blog/born-love/201003/touching-empathy.

3. Victor Hugo, *Les Misérables*, trans. Norman Denny, movie tie-in ed. (New York: Penguin, 2012).

4. Jason Silverstein. "There Were More Mass Shootings Than Days in 2019," CBS News, January 2, 2020, https://www.cbsnews.com/news/mass-shootings-2019-more -than-days-365/.

5. Jamie Smith, "Is red wine good for you?" *Medical News Today*, April 21, 2020, https://www.medicalnewstoday.com/articles/265635.

Chapter 5 The Gift That Costs Nothing

1. "Forgiveness: Your Health Depends on It," Hopkins Medicine, https://www .hopkinsmedicine.org/health/wellness-and-prevention/forgiveness-your-health -depends-on-it.

2. "Heart Disease Facts," Centers for Disease Control, https://www.cdc.gov/heart disease/facts.htm; "Heart Disease and Stroke Statistics—At-a-Glance," American Heart Association, https://www.heart.org/idc/groups/ahamah-public/@wcm /@sop/@smd/documents/downloadable/ucm_470704.pdf.

3. Everett L. Worthington, "Forgiveness, Health, and Well-Being: A Review of Evidence for Emotional versus Decisional Forgiveness, Dispositional Forgivingness, and Reduced Unforgiveness," *Journal of Behavioral Medicine*, September 2007, https://www.researchgate.net/publication/6376329_Forgiveness_Health_and_Well -Being_A_Review_of_Evidence_for_Emotional_Versus_Decisional_Forgiveness _Dispositional_Forgivingness_and_Reduced_Unforgiveness.

4. Pablo Diaz, "The Healing Power of Forgiveness," *Guideposts*, September 24, 2015, https://www.guideposts.org/better-living/positive-living/the-healing-power -of-forgiveness.

5. Bo Sanchez, *Awaken the Healer in You: How to Heal Your Body—God's Way!* (Quezon City, Phillipines: Shepherd's Voice, 2010).

6. "Psychro-," Etym Online, https://www.etymonline.com/word/psychro-.

Chapter 6 The Two Most Powerful Words on Earth

1. Aplana and Murari Chaudhuri, "Hormones and Neurotransmitters: The Differences and Curious Similarities," *The Biochemists*, June 26, 2018, https://medium.com /the-biochemists/hormones-and-neurotransmitters-the-differences-and-curious -similarities-46c6095b825.

2. Ann Pietrangelo, "How Does Dopamine Affect the Body?," Healthline, November 5, 2019, https://www.healthline.com/health/dopamine-effects.

3. Carrie D. Clarke, JD, ACC, "How Gratitude Actually Changes Your Brain and is Good for Business," Thrive Global, February 7, 2018, https://thriveglobal.com/stories /how-gratitude-actually-changes-your-brain-and-is-good-for-business/

Chapter 9 Let No One Take Your Crown

1. Quoted in Grenville Kleiser, *Dictionary of Proverbs* (New Delhi, India: APH Publishing, 2005), 141.

Chapter 10 Depressed No More

1. "350 million people have depression in world: WHO," Medical Press, October 9, 2012, https://medicalxpress.com/news/2012-10-million-people-depression-world .html.

2. "Depression Statistics," Depression and Bipolar Support Alliance, https://www .dbsalliance.org/education/depression/statistics/.

3. SingleCare Team, "Depression statistics," The Checkup, January 21, 2021, https://www.singlecare.com/blog/news/depression-statistics/.

4. "Mental Health in the Workplace," Anxiety & Depression Association of America, https://adaa.org/sites/default/files/Mental%20Health%20and%20the%20Work place%202017.pdf.

5. Ben Lesser, "Depression and Addiction: Symptons, Causes, Treatment," Dual Diagnosis.org, March 6, 2021, https://dualdiagnosis.org/depression-and-addiction/.

6. Faith Hope & Psychology, "80% of Thoughts Are Negative . . . 95% are repetitive," The Miracle Zone, March 2, 2012, https://faithhopeandpsychology.wordpress .com/2012/03/02/80-of-thoughts-are-negative-95-are-repetitive/.

7. "Gratitude Is Good Medicine," UC Davis Health, November 25, 2015, https:// health.ucdavis.edu/medicalcenter/features/2015-2016/11/20151125_gratitude .html.

Chapter 11 Shame Off You!

1. Erik H. Erikson, *Identity: Youth and Crisis* (New York: W. W. Norton, 1968), 112.

2. *The Edge* Sound Clips, accessed December 3, 2021, http://www.moviesound clips.net/sound.php?id=195.

3. Quoted in Lilith Regan, *Quotes by Carl Jung: The Complete Collection of Over 100 Quotes* (ind. pub., 2020), n.p.

Chapter 12 Anger

1. Smiljanic Stasha, "20+ Mind-Numbing U.S. Road Rage Statistics—2021 Edition," Policy Advice, February 26, 2021, https://policyadvice.net/insurance/insights/road-rage-statistics/.
2. Alan Mozes, "Almost 1 in 10 Americans has anger issues and access to guns, study finds," CBS News, April 8, 2015, https://www.cbsnews.com/news/1-in-10-americans-has-anger-issues-and-access-to-guns/.
3. "Angry Outbursts Appear to Boost Heart Attack, Stroke Risk," Harvard T. H. Chan School of Public Health, https://www.hsph.harvard.edu/news/hsph-in-the-news/angry-outbursts-may-boost-heart-attack-stroke-risk/.

Chapter 13 Free at Last

1. "Old & New Testament Greek Lexical Dictionary," https://www.studylight.org/lexicons/eng/greek/2390.html.
2. Quoted in *Barnes' Notes on the Bible*, "Isaiah 42:3," Bible Hub, accessed October 18, 2021, https://biblehub.com/commentaries/isaiah/42-3.htm.
3. Thomas Schreiner, "Was Luther Right?" Ligonier Ministries, https://www.ligonier.org/learn/articles/was-luther-right/.

Chapter 14 How to Stop Feeling Bad and Start Enjoying Life

1. Brand Minds, "The Health & Wellness Industry Is Now Worth $4.2 trillion," Manager Mint Media, April 25, 2019, https://medium.com/manager-mint/the-health-wellness-industry-is-now-worth-4-2-trillion-866bf4703b3c.

Chapter 15 You Are More

1. "You Are More," songwriters Michael Donehey/Jason Ingram. So Essential Tunes (SESAC) / Formerly Music (SESAC) / Spirit Nashville Three (formerly West Main Music) (SESAC) / (admin at EssentialMusicPublishing.com [3]). All rights reserved. Used by permission.

Chapter 16 Your Story Doesn't End Here

1. Derek Koza, "6 Famous Failures From Top Entrepreneurs," Data Driven Investor, March 10, 2019, https://medium.datadriveninvestor.com/6-famous-failures-from-top-entrepreneurs-c45d14e81355.
2. Dennis Nafte, "Colonel Sanders Failed 1009 Times Before Succeeding," Dennis Nafte, September 10, 2017, https://medium.com/@dennisnafte/colonel-sanders-failed-1009-times-before-succeeding-ac5492a5c191.
3. "Steve Jobs Grateful He Was Fired," Preaching Today, *Christianity Today*, http://www.preachingtoday.com/illustrations/weekly/05-08-15/stevejobsgratefulhewasfired.html; "Steve Jobs: Apple founder's moving speech on why being fired from tech giant was the best thing to happen," February 24, 2016, https://www.independent.co

.uk/news/people/steve-jobs-apple-founder-s-moving-speech-why-being-fired-tech
-giant-was-best-thing-happen-a6893196.html.

4. William Holland, "Living on Purpose: Considering the Cost," *The Sentinel*,
January 17, 2020, https://hanfordsentinel.com/living-on-purpose-considering-the
-cost/article_b61379f5-f3bb-5eab-8a39-72f7af9be1b5.html.

5. Tate Scholchinger, "He Bragged About Money to His Wife. How She Responds
Has Me Laughing Until I Wet Myself," *Greenville Gazette*, July 24, 2015, http://www
.greenvillegazette.com/p/68540/.

Continued from page 6.

Gregory Dickow was raised in a Middle Eastern family from Detroit, Michigan. As a young boy, Greg often felt like he was missing something in his life. Feeling lonely and unsure of himself, he began a heartfelt search for purpose in life after one of his closest high school friends unexpectedly committed suicide.

That tragedy, along with what he calls several divine turning points, would lead Greg to finally agree to go to a small Bible study for the first time with a friend from work. By the end of the study, he found himself inviting Jesus into his life. And by the end of that same night, he found himself sharing his newfound faith with a passion and confidence he had never known before. From that very moment, he began to experience God's beautiful unconditional love that has transformed his life and catapulted him into his life purpose—to introduce people to the real Jesus, empowering them to rise to their true worth and purpose, and to change mindsets that change the world.

In the early '90s, Greg, along with his wife, Grace, moved to Chicago and planted a different kind of church, where everyone would be welcomed—no matter their past—to discover God's grace; a place where everyone encounters the presence of God and the wealth of meaningful relationships. From humble beginnings in a rented grade school gymnasium, Life Changers International Church was born and began to grow.

In 1996, Greg led his new congregation, Life Changers, in the land acquisition and construction of their first campus on fourteen acres in Barrington Hills. In 2004, they built a 177,000-square-foot campus, more than tripling their capacity, on thirty acres in Hoffman Estates, Illinois. In 2016, after many years of meetings at Whitney Young High School in Chicago, Greg also led the acquisition and renovation of the 75,000-square-foot campus for Life Changers' downtown Chicago congregation.

Many know Greg as the author and creator of the global movement Fast from Wrong Thinking, which has been published in ten languages and experienced by nearly one million people, whose lives have been transformed through a systematic dismantling of wrong beliefs and mindsets.

What many may not know is, under Greg's leadership, Life Changers has grown into a global family—a church without walls, so to speak. Yet they have never waned in their commitment to local community outreach with feeding, education and evangelistic programs. They have a special focus on serving those in need, especially the fatherless, widows and the disenfranchised, by giving them hope, healing and practical care. At the same time, the church's international reach has expanded into over two hundred countries, with services translated into ten major languages.

What happened from the night Greg accepted Jesus, until now, is living proof that the God of all grace is a Father to the lonely, a Champion to the weary and a Friend to all who open the door of their heart to His loving company and His warm embrace.

You can connect with Greg in many ways:

Website: gregorydickow.com

Instagram: instagram.com/gregorydickow

TikTok: tiktok.com/music/original-sound-6964425948955577094

Facebook: facebook.com/gregorydickow

YouTube: youtube.com/user/powertochangetoday

Text (community number): (312) 313-8582

Podcast: anchor.fm/gregorydickow

Fast from Wrong Thinking: gregorydickow.com/fastfromwrong
    thinking